The GREAT Awakening

Testimonies of Jonathan Edwards
and George Whitefield

Mark C. Lee

Copyright @2021 by Mark C. Lee

All rights reserved. No part of this book may be reproduced in any form or by any electronic or mechanical means, including information storage and retrieval systems, without permission in writing from the publisher, except by reviewers, who may quote brief passages in a review.

This publication contains the opinions and ideas of its author. It is intended to provide helpful and informative material on the subjects addressed in the publication. The author and publisher specifically disclaim all responsibility for any liability, loss or risk, personal or otherwise, which is incurred as a consequence, directly or indirectly, of the use and application of any of the contents of this book.

WORKBOOK PRESS LLC
187 E Warm Springs Rd,
Suite B285, Las Vegas, NV 89119, USA

Website: https://workbookpress.com/
Hotline: 1-888-818-4856
Email: admin@workbookpress.com

Ordering Information:
Quantity sales. Special discounts are available on quantity purchases by corporations, associations, and others. For details, contact the publisher at the address above.

ISBN-13: 978-1-955459-14-3 (Paperback Version)
978-1-955459-15-0 (Digital Version)

REV. DATE: 24.03.2021

DEDICATION

To my mother, Dao-Ying Kao Lee; my wife, Mei-Lan; and my daughter, Nancy.

ACKNOWLEDGEMENTS

I am deeply indebted to my mentor, Audrey Silva, for her invaluable suggestions for my paper's outlines and wording; Qian Wu, for her time during the editing progress and generous help in the final self-publishing stages; and Jeanny Tsai, for her help in publishing this book.

TABLE OF CONTENTS

Introduction xiii
   Theme Verse Of This Book: (Psalm 19:7) xiii
   The Fundamental Role Of Prayer In Evangelism xiv
   The Intent And Scope Of This Book xv
   Methodology xix

1. The Church, The Great Commission, And Testimony 01
   Preaching And Its Authority 03
   Revivalism 07
   The Dawn Of The Great Awakening 09
   Arminianism Versus Calvinism 11
   Summary Of Chapter 1 39

2. Friendship Between The Wesley Brothers And Whitefield 42
   Whitefield's Conversion 45
   The Ministry Of Whitefield 48
   Theology Of The Great Awakening 60
   Whitefield's Roots Of Theology 73
   A Contrast Of John Wesley And Whitefield 78
   Summary Of Chapter 2 87

3. The Life And Ministry Of Jonathan Edwards 90
   Edwards's Conversion 91
   Edwards's Resolutions 94
   Edwards's Roots Of Theology 98
   Edwards's Impact On Wesley And Whitefield 101
   Summary Of Chapter 3 102

4. Leaders Of The First Great Awakening 108
Edwards's And Whitefield's Impact On The Great Awakening 109
New Milestones In Whitefield's Pulpit Preaching 113
Edwards's Preaching Style 122
The "New Lights" And The "Old Lights" 127
Summary Of Chapter 4 142

5. Legacies Of Edwards's And Whitefield's Testimonies 146
The Overall Effects Of The Great Awakening 171
Relationship Between The American Enlightenment And
     The Great Awakening 179
The Sovereignty Of God And The Free Will Of Humanity 181
Is It Too Late To Pray For Our Nation's Revival? 195

Final Thoughts 199
Bibliography 201
Vita 207
Concise Chronology 208

PREFACE

In the Great Awakening movement of colonial America in the eighteenth century, Jonathan Edwards and George Whitefield joined forces and made an enormous impact on the church and society. The movement was one of the most splendid spiritual revivals in the history of Christianity.

Beginning about 1720, a series of spiritual revivals started in England and came to America. The movement stirred up mass religious conversions among churches with a call for people to live holy lives.

Many responded; there were more people looking for churches to join Bible study fellowships. Leaders such as Edwards (1703–1758) promoted the establishment of schools to train people in ministry. Denominational colleges such as Princeton, Brown, and Dartmouth were founded to serve this need.

The movement is a historic lesson I confirmed in the preciousness of God's promise in 2 Chronicles 7:14 (all the Bible quotes in this book are from New King James Version, NKJV, unless otherwise noted): "If my people who are called by my name will humble themselves, and pray and seek My face, and turn from their wicked ways; then I will hear from heaven, and will forgive their sin and heal their land."

Edwards's lifelong testimony and high character are reflected his favorite verse: "I am the rose of Sharon, a lily of the valleys" (Song of Solomon 2:1).

One of the positive causes of his high character, and great success, as a preacher, was the deep and pervading solemnity of his mind. He had, at all times, a solemn Consciousness of the presence of God. From the first step to the last, he aimed at nothing but the salvation of his hearer and at the glory of God as revealed in it. This enabled him to bring all his powers of mind and heart to bear on this one object.

Whitefield's lifelong journey was the marvelous testimony of a faithful servant who followed the footsteps of our Lord to reach out to the sheep without shepherds. He has been credited with being the champion with his most dynamic ministry to plant the seeds of the gospel of salvation in the Great Awakening that swept across the British Isles and North America.

The impact Edwards and Whitefield left behind them was a great testimony and legacy of how God raised His faithful servants in a time of crisis.

INTRODUCTION

"Again I say to you that if two of you agree on earth concerning anything that they shall ask, it will be done for them by my Father in Heaven" (Matthew 18:19 NKJV). This verse is one of the great gospel promises with regard to prayer. The promise is particularly given to the church and all the disciples in joint prayers; praying communally will please God and unlock the door to receiving His promises and blessings.

Theme Verse of this Book: (Psalm 19:7)

The theme of this paper involves the perfect revelation of the Lord in this verse: "The *law* of the Lord is perfect, converting the soul; the *testimony* of the Lord is sure, making wise the simple" (Psalm 19:7).

Here, the *law* (H8451[1]) means the law, instruction, and direction (divine or human), the testimony, His law so-called because it is a witness between God and man. Every born-again Christian believes in the truth of the resurrection of Jesus Christ. Therefore, our purpose on earth is to testify to the truth of the words we received from the Holy Spirit carved and sealed on our souls. Jesus made it so clear when He said, "Search the Scriptures, for in them you think you have eternal life, and these are they which testify of me" (John 5:39) and "And this is the *testimony*: that God has given us *eternal life*, and this life is in His Son" (1 John 5:11).

---

[1] Warren Baker, D.R.E.; The Hebrew-Greek Key Study Bible 1991 Revised Edition; AMG Publlishers

The Fundamental Role of Prayer in Evangelism

We witnessed the early disciples in Acts 1:14: "These all continued with one *accord* in prayer and supplication, with the women and Mary the mother of Jesus, and with His brothers." The result of this prayer meeting was recorded in Acts 2:4: "And they were all filled with the Holy Spirit and began to speak with other tongues, as the Spirit gave them utterance" and "Then those who gladly received his word were baptized; and that day about three thousand souls were added to *them*" (Acts 2:41).

The spiritual awakening ever since the early apostles' days had its earthly origin in prayer. Edwards began with his famous call to prayer in the early eighteenth century and eventually started the Great Awakening.

My Motivation for Writing This Book

In 2008, I read a eulogy written by the famous American revolutionary poet Phyllis Wheatley (1753–1784) for Whitefield. Her writing touched my heart and led me to learn more about Whitefield to satisfy my curiosity about his life and legacy. Ms. Wheatley described the zealous spirit of Whitefield.

> He prayed that grace in every heart might dwell, He longed to see America cxcel: He charged its youth that every grace divine. Showed with full luster in their conduct shine; That Savior, which His soul did first receive, The greatest gift that even a God can give, He freely offered to the numerous throng, That on his lips with listening pleasure hung.

There were verses such as,

> Hail, happy saint, on thine immortal throne, Posses of glory, life and bliss unknown;

We hear no more the music of thy tongue, Thy wanted auditoriums cease to throng,

Thy sermons in unequalled accents flowed, and every bosom with devotion glowed;

Thou didst in strains of eloquence refined. Inflame the heart and captivate the mind.

There Whitefield wings, with rapid course his way, And sails to Zion, through vast seas of day. Washing in the Fountain of redeeming blood, You shall be son and kings, and priest to God.

Phillis Wheatley also took Whitefield as the subject of her first published poem: Whitefield, she wrote, preached "Take him, ye Africans, he longs for you, Impartial Savior is his title due."

The Intent and Scope of This Book

I started reading books about Whitefield's life and his ministry in 2008 and started expanding my reading to include his contemporary revivalist, Edwards, which eventually led to my study of the Great Awakening. The seeds of the awakening were sown in 1734 when Edwards was preaching revival sermons in Northampton, Massachusetts.

The essence of spiritual regeneration has to start with two key factors. First, new birth takes place by the action of the Holy Spirit, who can give life to those who were "Dead in trespasses and sins" (Ephesians 2:1). This new birth is often called the regeneration.

Second, the new birth must begin with the Word of God. "The law of the Lord is perfect, converting the soul; the testimony of the Lord is sure, making wise the simple" (Psalm 19:7).

We need to truly repentance and turn away from our sinful acts against God. We must first turn away from the corrupted way that was parting us from God's Commandments. Scripture warn us, "Every way of a man is right in his own eyes; but the Lord weighs the heart" (Proverbs 21:2).

God promised, "If my people who are called my name humble themselves, and turn from their wicked ways, and then I will hear from heaven and will forgive their sin and heal their land" (2 Chronicles 7:14).

My paper focuses on two of the great evangelists: Edwards and George Whitefield, their early family life, their ministry, and particularly how their lives have testified to their faith and impact on the church and the country.

Edwards and Whitefield dedicated their lives to honoring God in an awakening era and faithfully followed the Great Commission of the Lord.

It is my intention to explore how and why the Great Awakening can change the hearts of the thousands of believers and have an impact on all of society and how these two great evangelists' influence will help the church today.

What Is the Definition of *Revival*?

Hosea 14:2 mentions "revival": "Take words with you, and return to the Lord: say to Him, Take away all iniquity, receive us graciously, for we will offer the sacrifices of our lips." Christian revivals refer to specific period of increased spiritual interest or renewal in the life of a church or many churches.

> By the very structure of the word, revival means revivification of an existing church and members. There must first be tired believers before they can be revived. All accounts tell of cold, indifferent, or

sinful congregations that, by revival, are kindled to new consecration.

An awakening can be defined as a renewal of interest of interest in religion especially in community, church, and society.

> Revival is God's gift. Human being can neither command it nor make God grant it, God is sovereignty gives revival when and where he wills. Revival in the churches of Europe and America were preceded by long years of careful reading of the Bible in homes and churches. Christian revival would be impossible without knowledge of Christian Scriptures.

Religion could have an influence on people only if it touches souls that hear the true gospel: "So then Faith comes by hearing and hearing by the word of God" (Romans 10:17). Faith is rooted in believers' conviction respecting their relationship to God and divine things.

The Study of Religion

However, the notion of religion can be misleading. No belief is truly religious unless it exerts an impact on our lives. For many revitalized Christians, the distinctive mark of religion is not what they believe but how they believe. It is the bonfire of true Spirit itself energizing their commitment, loyalty, and devotion. To study religion helps us understand the beliefs and practices at a specific time.

Enlightenment and Pietism

The Enlightenment was preceded by the rise of Pietism in England, which led to the great evangelical revivals of the eighteenth century.

> In Germany, however, the Enlightenment followed

after the rise of Pietism, and thus developed in a situation which had been significantly shaped by religious faith, even if it would pose a serious challenge to the received forms and ideas of this faith. (Interestingly, English Deism began to become influential in Germany at roughly the same time as German Pietism began to exert influence in England.) The most significant intellectual forces in the German Enlightenment were thus directed toward the reshaping (rather than the rejection or demolition) of the Christian faith.

The church's revival history had its European origins; the European Pietism movement occurred between the 1690s and the early 1700s before spreading to England and the Netherlands.

One population factor was an increase in immigration.

After 1700, immigrants from England were greatly outnumbered by those from other countries. Foreign migration actually accounted for 25 percent of the colonial population growth between 1700 and 1775. This immigration grew out of religious conflicts and persecutions in the Old world.

The Pietism movement stressed personal religious introspection and the personal experience of true Christian transformation. Pietism developed in a number of directions especially in England and Germany. Among the representatives of the movement, two in particular should be noted— Nikolaus Ludwig Graf von Zinzendorf (1700–1760) and John Wesley (1703–1791).

Methodology

The historical approach involves checking all social, religious, and theological factors that contribute to the Great Awakening in colonial America and drawing clearer pictures of their individual contributions to the movement.

The approach of sociology of religion will help me use the findings from these articles and books and then analyze how Edwards's and Whitefield's roles contributed to social change. The biblical approach is the main source of my spiritual interpretation. Historical investigation aims at reexamining the revival movement and finding the reasons, factors, and forces behind this historical revival with a focus on the testimonies of the Great Awakening. The religious phenomena include myths, rituals, ways of thought, and most of all, the institutions in society at the time. C. H. Spurgeon (1834–1892) wrote,

> A true religion is the work of God: It's pre-eminently so. That God is indeed the author of salvation in the world and in the hearts of men, and that religion is the effect of grace, and is the work of God. As I (anyone) deny that one great Truth-the God is the author of good in the souls of men. It's also God's work-that in our souls which can carry us to heaven, (from first to last) we firmly believe that God who quickens the souls which has dead, positively. "Dead in trespasses and sins, that it is God who maintains the life of the soul."

> **Religious** man is magic-making man (Malinowski), fearing-man (Hume), and man directed toward the Unconditional (Tilich); he is man shuddering before manifestations of the numinous (Otto), devoting himself to and denying for the sake of universal ideal-energies (Dewey), like loving and dealing justly and other virtues ... man giving himself to transcendent beauty (Jonathan Edwards).

Three Elements of the Study of the Church: Time, Faith, and Forms

The sociological approach in the examination of the mid-eighteenth century American colonial churches' historical awakening movement required a great deal of research. I examined a great deal of material and engaged in analysis of it, including

1. the definitions of religion and the sociology of religion
2. the dawn of the Great Awakening
3. the roles these two evangelists contributed to the awakening
4. public comments from that era that covered their main theological roots

The Historical Approach to Fact-Finding

It's challenging to apply the historical approach to finding out the fact of the awakening era; it was a task to look into many mirrors of times past that are covered with layers of dust. I spent lots of time digging out facts from books, articles, letters, and sermons related to the subject of my study before I could decide which facts were useful in helping me see the clear picture of these historical events.

The Methodology of Sociology of Religion

The sociology of religion studies the interrelation and interaction of religion and society with special emphasis on the typology of religious groups. The goal of studying the sociology of religion is to come up with a descriptive sociological examination of religious groups.

The study of religions aims at understanding the meaning and purpose of religion in its various manifestations. Coupled with this study, I propose a system of classification of religions we need to bear in mind; it's not the formation of a scale starting with the religions of our opponents and ending with our own values.

The study of religion consists of different organizations, religious and secular. It comes naturally because the nature of religious study involves all kinds of organizations that always involve emotion, starting from our own individual feelings of dependence and ending with the organized forms of religion that we encounter in the history of humanity.

The Time of the Great Awakening

The Great Awakening occurred in the same era that Pietism started in the Netherlands and in Germany and the Wesleyan Revival in England, which constituted a reaction to the rationalism and secularism of the Enlightenment.

Enlightened Religion

> Fortunately, at the Awakening era, Jonathan Edwards, practically was the American Enlightenment-the first American to understand Locke's epistemology; and without the eighteenth-century Enlightenment, with its emphasis on reason, benevolence, tolerance, and progress, there would have been no Disestablishment of religion in America. Without it there would have been no escape from the theological monopoly that governments had always imposed, no rapid proliferation of the sects That multiplied as soon as Disestablishment occurred.
>
> It was a time when
>
> Most of the colonial were Protestants, devoutly committed to their various churches throughout the eighteenth century, for example, between 56 and 80 Percent of the colonial population participated

actively in the religious life of one or another denomination.

It is not surprising that the Enlightenment and Revivalism were mutually antagonistic in eighteenth-century America. But they did agree in rejecting earlier theocratic patterns, so that much as they differed in other respects, they both contributed to individualism and to the rise of religious liberty.

The fire of the Great Awakening that started with the Calvinistic Dutch Reformed and Presbyterians of the middle colonies soon spread to Congregationalist New England by the efforts of Edwards. The Great Awakening was an era of Protestant religious revivals that took place from the 1730s to the 1750s. My study concentrates on American colonies from the 1730s to 1740s and covers mainly Whitefield and Edwards.

Who Were the People of the Great Awakening Era?

Checking the historical information, I discovered that the majority of the colonies' populations in the mid-eighteenth century were the second and third generations of immigrants from Europe.

Amazing Grace

"Therefore know that the Lord your God, He is God, the faithful God who keeps covenant and mercy for a thousand generations with those who love Him and keep His commandments" (Deuteronomy 7:9). Abraham's faith was confirmed by his obedience and our gracious God: "For if God did not spare the natural branches, He may not spare you either" (Romans 11:21). We have a merciful God who expresses the worldwide applicability of the gospel. Gracious God Extends an Invitation to Abundant Life to Humankind "Ho! Everyone who thirsts, come to the waters; and you who have no money, Come, buy and eat. Yes, come, buy wine and milk without money and without price" (Isaiah 55:1).

God Created Humankind in His Own Image

The glory of the Lord in creation was described in Psalm 8:4–5: "What is man that You are mindful of him, and the son of man that You visit him? For You have made him a little lower than the angels, and You have crowned him with glory and honor."

God's promise is so clear in Isaiah 55:11 even after Adam's fall, He is concerned with pardoning even the greatest sinners. God's promises and words shall never return void. God's Will was carried out by the Work of Christ and confirmed by the Witness of the Holy Spirit that is sealed on believers' hearts. These three Ws remind me every day in our spiritual walk.

Our purpose in life must be to obey God and honor Him every day of our earthly walk.

Chapter 1

THE CHURCH, THE GREAT COMMISSION, AND TESTIMONY

Church

For Edwards, "the church was a reflection of God's eternal purpose. Before the world was created, the persons of the Holy Trinity entered into a 'covenant of redemption.'"

Looking at the time capsule of church history, whenever the church honors and obeys the Commandments of God, it will grow according to the will of God. At the same time, whenever the church disobeys and dishonors God, it will certainly lead to its fall.

God is always in full control of the fate of the church. In Psalm 18:28, God said, "For You will light my lamp; the Lord my God will enlighten my darkness."

The Great Commission

Jesus is the living testimony of the divine truth: "No man has seen God at any time. The only begotten Son, who is in the bosom of the Father, He has declared Him" (John 1:18).
The Father sent the Son to be the Savior of the world (1 John 4:14). Jesus' compassion for the multitudes was boundless.

But when He saw the multitudes, He was moved with compassion for them, because they were weary, and were scattered, like sheep having no shepherd. Then He said to His disciples, "The harvest truly is plentiful, but the laborers are few. Therefore Pray the Lord of the harvest to send out laborers into His harvest" (Matthew 9:37–38).

God also bearing witness both with signs and wonders, with various miracles, and gifts of the Holy Spirit, according to His own will. (Hebrews 2:4)

Philip Schaff (1819–1893) wrote a beautiful description of our Lord.

The image of Jesus: the image of the highest and purest, harmony both of his natural and his moral being. But as to Jesus, we all have the lively impression that here reigns perfect harmony of the absolute peace. He is all love, all heart, all feeling, and yet on the other hand, all in intellect, all clearness, all majesty, all in quiet greatness, peaceful simplicity, sublime harmony.

Evangelist

Evangelist is the name given to the New Testament heralds of salvation through Christ, the Redeemer of humankind. God's promise was made to Abraham and his descendants (his seed).

It means "teaching." It was not to his descendants but to his descendant; therefore, not all the people who were the descendants of Abraham were the heirs of promise, but only those who believed in his teaching. (Galatians 3:8)

> Evangelists answered the divine calling to serve the Lord and carry out the teaching of Christ in proclaiming the good tidings openly; they were called missionary preachers of the gospel (Ephesians 4:11).

Preaching and Its Authority

The perfect example is Philip in Acts 21:8; he traveled from city to city preaching God's Word (Acts 8:4, 40). Itinerant preachers carried the gospel to places where Jesus Christ was previously unknown.

The evangelists were followers of the Lord who committed themselves to witnessing and serving in passionate obedience to Jesus' Great Commission.

> Now all things are of God, who has reconciled us to Himself through Jesus Christ, and who has given us the ministry of reconciliation. Now then, we are ambassadors for Christ, as though God was pleading through us: we implore you on Christ's behalf, be reconciled to God. (2 Corinthians 5:18–20)

The apostle Paul was summing up the appeal he received from Christ that Jesus gave to the entire world. Reconciliation is the restoration of loving fellowship after estrangement. This is the true essence of the Great Commission.

The apostle Paul was an evangelist who followed the Holy Spirit to serve the Lord. With the mission-oriented ministry, Paul exhorts all of us.

The Duties of the Evangelist

To Proclaim the Glad Tidings

The evangelist is a missionary preacher who is to proclaim glad tidings; John 3:34 says, "For He whom God has sent speaks the words of God, for God does not give the Spirit by measure."

One example is of the obedience of Philip, who answered the angel of the Lord and spoke to him. Then he encountered the eunuch who began at the same Scripture and mentioned Jesus' humility of incarnation. The story ended with, "Both Philip and the eunuch went down into the water, and he baptized him" (Acts 8:29–38). Judging from the case of Philip, evangelists were called to be itinerant preachers, having the special function of carrying the gospel from place to place where the gospel was previously unheard of.

Paul made it clear in 1 Corinthians 2:4–5, "And my speech and my preaching were not with persuasive words of human wisdom, but in demonstration of the Spirit and of power, that your faith should not be in the wisdom of men but in the power of God." He explained further in verse 7, "But we speak the wisdom of God as in a mystery, the hidden wisdom which God ordained before the ages of our glory."

The Spirit guides the preachers to the hearers.

> But God has revealed them to us through His Spirit. For the Spirit searches all things, yes, the deep things of God. For what man knows the things of a man except the spirit of the man which is in him? Even so, no one knows the things of God except the Spirit of God. (1 Corinthians 2:10–11)

Carl Barth said it so well: "Preaching is therefore nothing other than the Word of God which he himself has spoken. Preaching is the essential miracle of proclamation, namely, that the word of God and speech become indissolubly linked."

To Be Watchmen

"Obey those who rule over you, and be submissive, for they watch out for your souls, as those who must give account. Let them do so with joy, and not with grief, for that would be unprofitable for you" (Hebrews 13:17).

To Carry Out the Great Commission

The Lord is the source of believers' spiritual strength. "I will put My Spirit within you, and cause you to walk in my statutes, and you will keep my judgments and do them" (Ezekiel 36:27).

My prayer for our beloved country, the United States of America, is God's words in Psalm 19:7–8.

> Teach us the perfect golden rule of reviving: The law of the Lord is perfect, converting the soul; The testimony of the Lord is sure, making wise the simple; The statutes of the Lord are right, rejoicing the heart; The commandment of the Lord is pure, enlightening the eyes. As the Spirit of God moves the hearts of His children, the Spirit shall move freely. And after the testimonies are verified and confirmed, the spiritual revivals will occur.

The Biblical Illustrations of Revivals

Revivals draw believers' hearts to identify with the suffering of Jesus Christ. "Whom have I in heaven but You? And there is none upon earth that I desire besides You. My flesh and my heart fail, but God is the strength of my heart and my portion forever" (Psalm 73:25–26).

It leads them to turn away from sin and toward holiness. "And having been set free from sin, you became the slaves of righteousness" (Romans 6:18).

It empowers their thirst for God's Words. "Oh that my ways were directed to keep your statutes! Then I would not be ashamed, when I look into all your commandments" (Psalm 119:5–6).

It inspires greater love for serving the Lord and serving one another. "Yet it shall not be so among you; but whoever to become great among you shall be your servant: And whoever of you desires to be first shall be slave of all" (Mark 10:43–44).

Religion and Its Sociological View

"On the surface, religion in American history appears to be characterized by a rhythmic ebb and flow of vitality."

The logical way to study the subject of religious beliefs, practices, and attitudes starts with a concise definition of *religion*. In *Cultural Anthropology*, Dr. William A. Haviland wrote,

> Religion is an organized system of idea about spiritual reality, or the supernatural, along with associated beliefs and ceremonial practices by which people try to interpret and control aspects of the universe otherwise beyond their control.

The sociology of religion is a social science study of the interrelation and interaction of religion and society with a special emphasis on the typology of religious groups. The study of the sociology of religion is limited to a descriptive sociological examination of religious groups, and it is focused on presenting material that provides the philosophical convictions and persuasions of particular religions.

The aim of the study of religions is to understand the meaning and purpose of religion in its various manifestations. Coupled with the study, I propose a system of classification for religions. But we need to keep in mind that this is not the formation of a scale starting with the religions of our opponents and ending with our values. The nature of religion involves emotion, starting from our feeling of dependence for organized forms that we encounter in the history of humanity.

In his *Anthropology* for Christian Witness, Charles H. Kraft stated,

God wants to act in today's societies very much like He acted among the Hebrews and later in the Greek world, as portrayed in the Bible. I believe God is pro-culture, though anti-sin and anti-the satanic use of a people's customs ... What, then, should our attitude be toward the religion of a people? In keeping with the definition of religion given above, I believe it should be virtually the same as our attitude toward the rest of the culture. In this area, however, we need to be especially concerned about allegiance and empowerment.

With respect to the allegiance, we must maintain that people are saved or lost on the basis of whether or not their primary commitment is to the true God. Whatever the secondary allegiances, ritual, other beliefs and practices may be they are of much less importance than the primary allegiance.

With regard to empowerment, the facts are, "Dedication of cultural practices and implements to gods and spirits has been a regular part of 'Pagan' religions and often of other aspects of pagan cultural life as well."

Dr. Kraft firmly stated, "Allegiance to Christianity is not saving, as Allegiance to God is. What is more, that system, which its beliefs, practices, rituals, And organizations are not worth giving our life for."

Revivalism

Revivalism based on the Scriptures may be illustrated by Pietism and Methodism in the Lutheran and Anglican Churches. In addition to its infusion of fresh spiritual vigor into the Lutheran church, Pietism resulted in the founding of the Moravian church by Count Nicholas von Zinzendorf (1700–1760); he had a great influence on John Wesley.

In the conviction of spiritual revival, regeneration, or conversion, religious faith is manifest through the believers in making the person or group start the faith transformation process. "So then faith comes by hearing and hearing by the word of God" (Romans 10:17).

The gospel is proclaimed by preachers at congregations and religious gathering places. The power of the Holy Spirit works upon the hearers' hearts and leads them in the process from conversion to regeneration. The Spirit of the truth touches the souls of converts to begin the miracle of new birth, that is, the making of a sinner holy and expressing the fact that God's agency induces the change.

Adoration of Edwards and Whitefield

Edwards's "A Treatise Concerning Religious Affections" (1746) originated from sermons that provided a careful analysis of how to distinguish true religious affections from sensational excess. He wrote that his new sense was not "a new faculty of understanding, but a new kind of exercise of the same faculty of understanding."

He emphasized the importance of the role of heart and affections in religious life. For him, true religion involved rationality and included the intellect and understanding, but most of all, it had to include the will, and the affections motivated the heart toward what the will would choose.

Revivals have occurred many times during the Dark Ages as well as in Protestant North America. It occurred in times of crisis; God mandated through the Holy Spirit to bring believers to their knees and repent of their sins.

Among many faithful servants who answered the call from God

for repentance were Edwards and Whitefield (1714–1770), two of the foremost preachers in American Christian church history.

I was fascinated for years by these two great evangelists; I quoted their stories almost at every sermon I prepared. My spirit was inspired every time I quoted from their great sermons. These two evangelists were the spark plugs who made a huge impact on American church history. Historians have credited them as the catalysts of the Great Awakening.

Studying their family histories, diaries, sermons, and writings allowed me to trace their roots of spirituality as well as their differences and great testimonies.

The Dawn of the Great Awakening

The Pilgrims sailed to America on the Mayflower and established a settlement at Plymouth Colony on December 21, 1620. The Puritans established the Massachusetts Bay Colony in 1629; they sought to reform the Anglican Church by forming a pure church in the New World. Their numbers grew in two years from 400 to over 2,000.

The Colonial Background of the Era

The cultures of the early eighteenth century's colonies were very complex. The class similarities among farmers and gentlemen merged into a consolidated class culture.

Ethnic differences were transformed by various economic uses colonists made of this country. American farmers persistently grew different crops with different forms of labor. The minority of women gained some rights in the north but none in the south. Regional differences within class cultures had a profound effect on the lives of the American people.

The Puritan colonies' officials were elected by their communities;

only white males who were Congregationalists could vote. This was a far cry from our modern standards of democracy. These elected officials were not responsible to their local people. Their main function was to serve God best by overseeing the moral and physical improvement of the community. In a way, it seems like the political liberality of today.

Under the Massachusetts charter of 1691, Puritans were forced to allow freedom of worship. As a result, since the early seventeenth century, the Puritan church began to weaken its grip on the colonists. The new charter also banned the practice of permitting only Puritan church members to vote.

> By the 1730s and 1740s Puritanism had weakened considerably in New England. Congregational or Presbyterian churches stood at the centers of every city and town, but their influence had dwindled. Most citizens were not faithful followers of original Puritan ideals, and the grip of the Puritan preachers on the reins of civil power had loosened. Whereas the original New England Puritans had sought to avoid the curse of "mixed Assemblies" (churches where true believers and unbelievers mingled), it had invaded their churches in the early and mid-eighteenth century.

Edwards sought to reverse this trend with evangelistic fervor. He also brought his spiritual discipline and strong Christian intellect to this endeavor. Unfortunately, it was too late despite his fighting spirit to return the New England Puritanism to its first love. Edwards became the greatest Puritan theologian to defended Puritan Calvinist doctrines against the "creeping" Arminianism thought of his times. The emphasis of evangelism and the new birth that eventually fueled the Great Awakening underscored the churchgoers' diminished bond with the old routine.

Arminianism versus Calvinism

Arminianism

Here is the comment of TULIP to the vocabulary of Reformed theology.

1. Total depravity of sinful nature
2. Unconditional election (humans are not predestined)
3. Limited atonement (Christ died for only the elect)
4. Irresistible grace (by which the elect are infallibly called and redeemed)
5. Perseverance of the saints (those who are truly predestined by God cannot in any way defect from that calling)

Calvinism

> An ambiguous term, used with two quite distinct meanings; first, it refers to the religious ideas or religious bodies (such as Reformed church) and individuals who were profoundly influenced by John Calvin, or by documents written by him. Second, it refers to John Calvin's religious idea itself. Although the first sense is by far more common, there is a growing recognition that the term is misleading.

Background of the Colonial Church

In New England as in England, Puritan worship was quite lengthy. It typically consisted of an opening prayer, a reading from the Bible, psalm singing, a sermon, another singing of a psalm, a prayer, and a concluding blessing. The service frequently lasted three to four hours.

The New England Puritans were considered the founders of the church due to their generally higher economic standing and standard of living. Town leaders in New England could literally rent out their towns' impoverished families for a year to anyone who could afford them as a form of alms or cheap labor.

> By 1700 American Protestantism appeared to be stagnant. The first generation of Puritan immigrants was possessed with a driving religious vision that was not always shared by their children. Church membership began to decline. When increased immigration from Europe led to the Middle Atlantic States becoming religiously diverse to an extent without parallel anywhere else, awkward questions were raised about earlier Puritan visions of a "holy commonwealth." More significantly, a series of scandals rocked the credibility of Puritan institutions. The worst of these were the *Salem witch trials of 1693*: instigated by the clergy of that town, that led to the execution of nineteen people. George Sir William Phips eventually put an end to the hysteria, and the subsequent clerical apologies and recantations seriously diminished the standing and reputation of the clergy of the area.

Each church assembly was subject to the authority of a colonial governor and his council of ministers, who had the right to veto laws on behalf of the British government. The emerging new spirit from the different denominational churches was welcome. However, the spiritual condition of the colonies' established churches continued under the influence of Europe's states churches but could not compel taxpayers to tithe any more after the late seventeenth century to attend their service.

> Most of the colonists were *Protestants*, devoutly committed to their various churches. Throughout the eighteenth century, for example, 56 and 80 percent of the colonial population participated

actively in the religious life of one or another denomination.

In the early 1720s, the voice of a crusade for religious liberty was backed by two well-known Anglican organizations, the Society for the Propagation of the Gospel and the Society for the Propagation of the Christian Knowledge in New England. This started the raging fire of Puritanism. It broke out at the time because majority of church members attended meetings, listened to sermons or fell asleep during them, and kept holy only on the Sabbath. Many fell away from the church; they were simply going through the motions.

The Church in New England

Puritanism began in England most visibly as an effort to reform the nature of worship. What went on in the churches of the nation seemed to the *Puritan* still too Catholic, too "Papist". Worshippers should not kneel when receiving the sacrament at the communion (or Eucharist or Lord's Supper) for that suggested a kind of idolatry, an acceptance of the Catholic idea that the wine and the bread were in fact transformed into the body and blood of Jesus Christ. Vestments should not be worn that implied a spiritual distance between clergy and laity as if those persons belonged to the separate castes.

The family was the most important unit of society in colonial America. Communities in the New World were quite small at first, and for a long time they remained relatively small compared with the same cities and towns today. A person often was related by blood or marriage to nearly every family in his or her village. Those close relationships connected colonial people to one another in a network of close bond. Many people in the colonies also lived and worked under an arrangement called *indentured servitude*. Under this arrangement, in exchange for passage to the New World, a person agreed to work in the colonies as a servant for a period of years. Indentured servants often were treated brutally, but ultimately they received completed freedom. Even among the dour Puritans and Pilgrims, colonial life played an important role. Being so accustomed to death and hardship, people embraced chances to celebrate. Within a parish, a birth or wedding was always causing for celebration.

People also gathered for harvest festivals, holiday feasts, and other large parties. In the colonies there was little spare time apart from work, but work often was combined with play. Festivities accompanied the hard work. Social events included everyone in a community; activities were not segregated by chronological age or generation.

In 1733, Georgia was the last founded of the colonies. With the early traditional spirit of righteousness, Georgia attracted John and Charles Wesley in transplanting Methodism in America.

The First Permanent Settlement of the Moravians in 1740

By the Wesley's invitation came eloquent Whitefield, who devoted his life to spreading Calvinist vision from Georgia to Massachusetts and across the colonies. The decade (1740–1750) witnessed Moravian activity in the colonies, with the objective of spreading gospel and converting the Native population of the Delaware.

Material comfort had also weakened the Puritans' strict code. This factor had further attributed to the decline in church membership. Even the preachers seemed gradually to lose their interest in serving. The church was in the state of spiritual sleep. As a result, many religious people were ready for a religious awakening.

Despite the continuing differences and the persistence of colonial loyalties, a new, rich, socially elite group with a new cultural pattern was established on the rise of hereditary fortunes in every colony. As this trend continued, politics developed; public life after 1720s became much more settled across the colony.

> Only in Virginia and in New England did a parish system, designed to embrace a total community, function with any real degree of success. In Virginia the success was limited. The pattern of settlement in Virginia was a major problem. With the population thinly distributed on large plantations boarding the navigable rivers, a single parish could be from thirty to one hundred mile in length. In such a situation, it was difficult for the parish incumbent even to keep in touch with the parishioners, to say nothing of maintaining regular service of worship and a systematic program of instruction for them. In New England the pattern of settlement on small landholdings gathered about a village center was more conducive to an effective parish system and it was maintained largely unimpaired until the inroads of dissent destroyed the religious homogeneity of the population.

One of the evangelic preachers who tried to promote the revival was Edwards of the Congregational church in Northampton, Massachusetts. Edwards warned that people would not enter eternal life just by attending church services and praying. He

THE GREAT AWAKENING

declared that church people had to do more; they had to recognize the sinfulness of their lives and open their hearts to God's Spirit for repentance and conversion.

> The new emphasis on individuals having undergone a personal conversion led to the emergence of "conversion narratives" as a means of proving religious commitment and affirming personal identity.... So how such a revival might be accommodated within the confines of a Calvinist theology? How could such an experiential approach to the religious life be reconciled with the theological logic of a movement often associated with intellectual rigor rather than devotional fervor? The answer lies in the dynamic of theological internalization-the process by which ideas are transmuted into attitudes. The capacity of contemporary Puritanism to forge links between theology and experience must be regarded as one of its most significant characteristics, and above all in relation to explaining the origins of the Great Awakening.
>
> Puritanism is an excellent instance of a movement which placed theological integrity alongside pastoral applicability believing that each was incomplete without the other. The writings of individuals, such as Richard Baxter and Jonathan Edwards are saturated with the belief that theology finds its true expression in pastoral care and the nurture of Souls.

The Newspapers and Educational System

> Some developments were laying the groundwork for a sense of inter-colonial community and

cooperation. The increase of population produced an almost continuous line of settlement along stretches of the coast, and this brought the people of different colonies into closer contact. So did new roads, the rise of trade, and improvements in the colonial post office. By the mid-eighteenth century, the postal service extended all the way from New Hampshire to Georgia. Post riders carried newspapers as well as letters, and this enlarged and unified the colonial reading public.

The first newspaper of the colony, the *Boston-News Letters*, was published starting in 1704 on a regular basis and was circulated around Boston. The major colonial's newspaper of the awakening era was the *Colonial Times,* which covered a wide range of topics and was written for the most educated people in the country.

In colonial America in the 1730s, the Bible was considered the most influential book, the Word of God that was easily accessible to the public. The middle colonies had no laws requiring the public support of schools. However, various Calvinist churches did require their members to learn how to read.

The cultures of colonial America were very complex. By the mid-eighteenth century, class similarities between city gentlemen and rural farmers pointed toward consolidated class cultures. The major trait of ethnic differences transformed by varying economic uses colonists made of the American environment persisted.

The Social Background of the Era

The term *colonial* term originally came from British English; it meant *inferior*. Virginia, part of the Chesapeake colonies, was an inauspicious beginning for England's first region of permanent settlement on the North American mainland. In the eighteenth century, Maryland imported substantial numbers of British convicts as bound laborers usually for terms of seven years, but again, the supply fell short of the demand.

Slavery became the solution to this problem of the shortage of labor. In Virginia and Maryland, the shift to imported African slave labor began; this gradually changed the whole picture of the agricultural style of society in the following years before the awakening era.

In Virginia and Maryland, the leading social classes were the planters and their associates of merchants and lawyers, though the roles often overlapped. They were the forces who moved from place to place for new opportunities. They were looking for better lives both materially and spiritually. Some English immigrants went back and stayed in England, where they provided needed capital that was called *adventures*, a word that still echoes in today's *venture capitalist*.

The Growing Socio-Economic Distinction between the Colonial North and South

Farming was the major activity across the colonies at that time; however, things started to change in the north as the banking, shipping, fishing, and manufacturing industries gained more weight in urban settings such as Boston, New York, and Philadelphia. These three cities eventually become financially and culturally significant.

The divergence between the north and south was fueled by class cleavage that ran through the colonies. The twofold cleavage, regional and social, had increasingly challenged the Christian movement.

The plutocracy later gradually dominated both houses of the legislatures, the local governments, the colonial militias, and the church vestries. By the early eighteenth century, it was natural for the colonial people to seek their own identities. The result was that the colonies founded their own councils.

Eventually, the growth of the colonies' diverse populations changed the picture for the church: new congregations—the Anglicans and the Lutherans—came to America, and the Puritans' influence started to decline. Unfortunately, not all European churches supported the idea of religious freedom.

North America was being taken over by Anglo-Saxon civilization and becoming a place where the population continued to increase. For a long time, the spirit of Puritan pride had instilled an incredible ingredient into the colonial Americans' national character in history.

History of the Colonial Church

The Church of England was established in Virginia, Maryland, most of New York, the Carolinas, and Georgia by British colonial law. The law required each colonial church to pay taxes for financing the local Anglican church regardless of belief or affiliation.

Other than the Separatists of Plymouth, the Puritan founders of Massachusetts had arrived at their own intention of not breaking away from the Church of England. However, they insisted on the independent right to choose congregations' ministers and establish internal church structures. They finally arose in Massachusetts and Plymouth and became known as the Congregational Church.

> Not all the Puritans were Congregationalists; some of them became Presbyterians. In belief, these two groups were essentially the same. Both were Calvinists-believers in the doctrines of French Protestant John Calvin. According to Calvin's teachings, every soul is predestinated either for

salvation or for damnation. Those persons whom God has chosen to save-the "elect" –can be expected to give evidence of their future glory by the upright, moral life they live in this world. Though similar in theology, the Presbyterians and the Congregationalists differed in church organization. The Presbyterians had a more highly centralized government, with a governing body of presbyters (made up ministers and lay elders) for the churches of each district. The member of Presbyterians in America was greatly increased by the immigration of the Scotch Irish.

The Key Social Factors of Population Growth

The colonial population grew rapidly in the eighteenth century from 250,000 in 1700 to 2.5 million in 1775. Two key factors are attributed to its growth: natural increase and immigration. Since the 1700s, immigrants from England outnumbered immigrants from other European countries three to one.

The tide shifted in the eighteenth century due to the immigration of Scotch-Irish immigrants. They were pushed out to the edge of the wilderness because of their Presbyterian religion.

In the late eighteenth century, the most homogenous and most purely English part of the colonies was New England. The most cosmopolitan area was Pennsylvania; its English, German, and Scotch-Irish made up thirds of the population.

The Changing Pictures of Colonial Churches

Throughout the first two centuries, the Puritans settled in colonial America. The immigrants from Europe were seeking new identities for themselves. That occurred against the backdrop of the inheritances most European colonists brought with them. They identified with the Anglicans who settled the southern colonies and established the Church of England, or they identified with Puritan Protestants who, rebelling against the Church of England, came to the northern colonies to be free to establish their own congregational churches.

The Ruling Bodies of the Colony

To become acquainted with the historical development of the Great Awakening Era, we have to begin with the colonial society's ruling structure to gain a clearer picture of the era.

The eight royal colonies of America in the mid-eighteenth century were governed by British governors, colonial councils, and assemblies. The governors were the executive officers who were appointed by the British government. The council members served as the advisory board and the upper house of the legislature; the council members were also appointed by the British government. The assembly members were elected by the colony's property owners; it functioned as the lower house of the legislature.

Collision Course of the Churches

What was the spiritual condition of colonial churches in the 1730s? As the churches' influence and function were declining in society, many Christian missionaries and evangelists were quite discouraged; their morale hit a low point. The overall spiritual situation of the churches was negative, and many members of different denominations were desperately hoping for reform.

The era of the awakening was at the highlight of human civilization; it occurred in the same era that Pietism was popular in the Netherlands and in Germany while the Wesleyan movement started in England. The so-called new learning was influenced

THE GREAT AWAKENING

by the Enlightenment, and combined with the climate of intense religious enthusiasm, public sentiment, and thinking of that time, became complicated.

The colonies owed to these pioneers a new birth of spirit that had been an outgrowth of the Pietism of Europe and of the Puritanism and Evangelicalism of the British Isles.

As the time moved on, the Great Awakening brought a tradition of religious revivalism to America.

> The form of the Enlightenment that prevailed in the United States was derived from an important school of Scottish thinker known as "common sense" philosophers. Guided by the moralist Francis Hutcheson (1694–1745) and general work of Thomas Reid (1710–96), these Scots shared the general confidence of eighteenth-century Europe. It was now possible to see the truth-moral, physical, social-with greater clarity than in previous generations. They differed from other thinkers such as *Hume* and *Voltaire* by showing how their Enlightenment thought could be compatible with at least the broad outline of received Christianity. Proponents of common-sense philosophy held that it was "realistic" because it asserted that humans could genuinely know true things about the world outside their minds. Americans found the Scottish philosophy useful in three ways: (1) For justifying the Revolution against British. (2) For outlining new principles of social order in the absence of the stability British rule, and (3) For reestablishing the truth of Christianity in the absence of an established church.

New Sprouts of the New Branch of the Old Tree

The decay of the churches' function (lacking the fire) to satisfy the spiritual needs of its changing members of different congregations was perhaps the single most vital factor that led to the Great Awakening. The beginnings of congregationalism dated back to 1581 in a church in Norwich, England.

The Congregational establishment continued over the next two centuries to rally the support in the legislature for independence from outside interference. The Congregational Church was the major force until challenged by the disruptive religious enthusiasm released in the eighteenth-century's Great Awakening. Anglican Rev. Robert Browne and his followers were forced to move to Holland and then to America, where as the Mayflower Pilgrims, they landed at Plymouth, Massachusetts, in 1620.

Roger Williams was banished later from Massachusetts in 1636 and soon founded the colony of Rhode Island with an unusual extension of religious freedom.

In the 1720s, the malodorous Jacobus Frelinghuysen came to America, where he was shocked by the conventional and formal worship style. His "revivalism" roots helped to lead his parishioners to take more seriously the spiritual inwardness of Calvinism.

The preaching of Frelinghuysen was the first new breeze that arrived in the Dutch Reformed Church in Raritan Valley, New Jersey. His preference was practice in Pietistic fashion and insisted on a personal experience of conversion that led to moral transformation.

> Under Frelinghuysen, the Raritan church's revival reached its peak in 1729 and spread to other Dutch Reformed Churches. Frelinghuysen also preached, even in his early days, sermons which are more typical of later revivalistic preaching, with fervent

emotional warnings and appeals often addressed directly to the hearer as an individual.

God sent William Tennent (a Presbyterian pastor who was Irish born) to America in 1716. He was a saint with a vision to train young men for the divine mission of salvation. Tennent diligently trained the first group of seven students at the Log College (later Princeton University). These students became the preachers dedicated to the great revivalist cause of the awakening.

William's son Gilbert was a pastor in New Brunswick, New Jersey, where he preached widely as an itinerant. He became a close friend of Frelinghuysen and Edwards. Tennent, Whitefield, and Edwards were called the big three of the Enlightenment.

In the early 1730s, the secularized Congregational churches had started shunning many members; this eventually caused a reaction that spread among churchgoers.

Edwards began preaching an awakening in 1734 that had wide echoes in America and England. For Edwards, the revival was a sign of God's grace rather than a means of obtaining it.

He was at first well-disposed to the Great Awakening, which began soon afterward, but he drew back from its excesses. He was concerned primarily with the pastoral duty of counseling souls to understand and accept God's grace working on them; he was never a mere revivalist seeking to make converts.

In his book *The Distinguishing Marks of a Work of the Spirit of God* (Boston, 1741), Edwards sought to distinguish between a primary divine inspiration and a secondary human response. To Edwards, the true "distinguishing marks of the work of the spirit" were ultimately judged by holiness; the attachment of the affections to all that was godly.

In Edwards's Some *Thought & a Answering the Present revival in New England* (Boston, 1742), he attempted to distinguish true piety from the false and to defend the revival movement in its widest sense as a genuine work of the Holy Spirit.

The Pluralism of Church Development

Colonial America was a blessed soil for accepting the religious pluralism that required the spiritual toleration to accept a different breed of unique accommodation in the polity of the new nation. The religious establishment designated particular religious groups or denominations as favored by local civil authorities that allowed public revenues to support the clergy.

By 1730, the Congregational churches had become very thoroughly secularized. As a result, this induced a very strong reaction called the Great Awakening ushered in by Edwards.

New Leadership in Churches

Many great preachers came to colonial America and ignited the fire of this era. In colonial churches with a tradition of lay independence on religious matters, any clergy who ignored their flocks' spiritual needs ran a grave risk of being rejected in favor of others who preached more meaningfully. During the early 1700s, such was the case, and situations slowly developed.

The leadership of most religions at that time fell to senior clerics whose religious training at Harvard, Yale, or European universities had taught them to preserve orthodoxy by defending their denominations' theological positions through highly learned but dry and tedious sermons. They judged candidates for the ministry primarily on their scholarly knowledge rather than on their spiritual commitment or ability to inspire a congregation to recognize the need for moral regeneration in their own lives.

By the 1720s, too many if not most Americans were under the charge of a pedantic clergy who bored them with dull sermons, scolded them for their sins, and made Sunday services a stale, impersonal experience.

A new group of fresh, spirited clergy gradually stood out among the ministers; members of this new breed gradually emerged among the clergy with a direct, extemporaneous style of preaching that would prick their listeners' consciences. This is best described in John 16:8: "And when the Comforter is come, He will convict the world of sin, and of righteousness, and of judgment."

During most of the awakening era, these preachers demonstrated their visions to disgust their listeners with sin's loathsomeness, and in many cases, they were led to accept salvation through grace.

What Do Historians Say about the Great Awakening?

The Great Awakening's main characteristic was the religious enthusiasm of the Protestants that swept the colonies between the 1730s and 1740s. Historians have distinguished the Great Awakening with the label of revivalism, the spiritual revival that not only changed the churches but also affected the life of the colonies.

Theologian John Cobb observed Christianity as a mirror in which to look for continuity in a group's self-identification as a community of memory rather than an unchanging essence. He wrote,

> The unity of Christianity is the unity of a historical movement. That unity does not depend on any self-identity of doctrine, vision of reality, structure of existence or style of life. It depends on demonstrable continuities, the appropriateness of creative change, and the self-identification of people in relation to a particular history.

As the new revivalism spread across the colonies, not all the churches' servants—lay or clergy—embraced it. As the result of the different responses, three parties—anti-revivalists, moderates, and radicals—were formed. However, the interdenominational character of the awakening could not be denied. Various ecclesiastical bodies and religious groups were affected by great preachers such as Edwards at home and John Wesley and Whitefield overseas.

The network of awakeners drew the colonies together. The revivals also broke down some class barriers and democratized church life. It also contributed a great deal to missionary, educational, and humanitarian activities.

These great orators' sermons demonstrated their extreme expressions of emotionalism that were regarded as typical of revival religion in general.

> The awakening was preached by Dutch Reformed men like Theodorus Frelinghuysen, Presbyterians like William Tennent and his sons, Anglicans like George Whitefield, and Congregationalists like Jonathan Edwards. The seeds of the Awakening were sown in New Jersey, where fresh winds of piety were carried from Westphalia by Theodorus Jacobus Frelinghuysen, from Scotland and Ireland by William Tennent and Gilbert Tennent.

At the beginning, the outpouring of religious fervor was welcomed by some pastors. When the crowds spilled into fields and streets for regular Sunday church services, the clergies of traditional congregations were overshadowed and they began their severer thoughts.

> The collective protest of the Great Awakening movement led certain individuals and groups into session. That, however, was more the exception

than the rule. The vehement controversies over the character and value of the revival movements "particularly over the extraordinary exercise accompanying them" which continued for so long after they subsided, shows that, even if separation did not occur to any considerable extent, the question of the limit of the orthodox and heterodox, the permitted and the illicit, was definitely put and eagerly discussed in the various denominations affected by the revival "Baptists, Methodists, Presbyterians.

The anti-revivalist forces were critical of these new spiritual movements. They were afraid of the dangers and never ceased to address their extreme concerns about the revivalists' overenthusiasm.

Among the throngs of moderate evangelicals, however, the revival's new spirit was welcomed but with a cautious, wait-and-see attitude.

Preachers from many denominations were represented in the awakening era. Revivals and revivalists stirred audiences with vivid accounts of human sinfulness and urged them to see the need for redemption. Many claimed to have had conversion experiences at these meetings and said that their lives were never the same.

The Greek word for gospel is *evangel*, glad tidings, good news, welcome information, a shout, or something that makes people sing, talk, or rejoice. When David defeated Goliath, there was a great shout and an encouraging message was passed among the Jews to say that their terrible enemy had been killed and that they were free to enjoy liberty and peace. They sang, danced, and made merry at the news.

The gospel is God's power being manifest by the Holy Spirit through the humanity of Jesus. The good news is that God still manifests Himself by the Holy Spirit through our humanity today.

Colossians 3:16 tells us, "Let the words of Christ dwell in you richly in all wisdom teaching and admonishing one another in psalms and hymns and spiritual songs, singing with grace in your hearts to the Lord."

John Wesley pointed out this verse by emphasizing,

> Let the words of Christ-so the Apostle calls the whole scripture, and thereby asserts the divinity of his master. Dwell-not make a short stay, or an occasional visit, but take up its steady residence. With richly- in-largest measure, and with greatly efficacy; so as to fill and govern the whole soul.

The key issue of revival is confirmed once again; it rested on the work of the Holy Spirit. As long as the church teaches faithfully the truth of Christ's words, the revival will be genuinely empowered from the above and not be prompted by a counterfeit spirit. William Pitt (1708–1778), the Earl of Chatham, said it well: "We have a Calvinistic creed, a Popish liturgy, and an Arminian clergy."

Unlike today, the religious events and movements of colonial peoples were recorded in the headlines of newspapers and in books and memories as they were passed down from grandparents to grandchildren among Christian families.

Colonial America had been under the rule of Great Britain since 1607 in Jamestown, Virginia; that rule ended in 1776. The settlement of most of North America came after England's Reformation. The Spanish, French, English, Dutch, and Swedish colonies in North America were the outposts of European Christianity; this was a new, long, experimental process to transplant various cultural branches across a complex colonial spectrum.

The majority of people in colonial America during the awakening era were the second and third generations of European colonialists. But to the Englishmen and some of the European immigrants, their attitude toward slavery was tough. The prejudice was quite common against African Americans; the good thing was that most of the colonists thought that they consequently could be saved. African Americans were gradually accepted by Christianity.

Not all colonial whites accepted the legitimacy of slavery. A number of Puritans, Quaker, and other devout Christians argued earnestly against it. The most eloquent of the antislavery reformers was a New Jersey Quaker, John Woolman. He wrote a moving book, *Some Considerations on Keeping of Negroes* (published in 1754 and 1762), and traveled through the South to visit slaveholding Quakers and try to convince them that slave-holding was a sin.

Branch of Puritanism

Although Puritanism was a major theological and political force in early seventeenth-century England, the repressive religious policies of King Charles forced many Puritans to leave England. Puritans in the early seventeenth century did not stay with its pure, original Calvinism; instead, they shifted to the rationalistic links with cosmology and faith.

> The real *Calvinism* is the teachings linked to John Calvin of 16th century. Calvin's theology paved of the way of "salvation through Jesus Christ was accepted by people who were Anglicans; such as many of the puritan party in the church of England; including bishops such as George Abbot, Edwin Sundays, and James Davenant; by independents (or Congregationalists) such as the puritan John Owen; and Baptists such as *John Bunyan*. They willingly accepted Calvin's teaching on the way of salvation but declined his views on church government and on church and state. One Greek Orthodox theologian,

Cyril Lucaris, patriarch of Constantinople, even wrote a Calvinistic Confession in 1629, but the Orthodox Church later rejected it. That was the *first seismic* change. The *second* was the effect on Calvinists of the first tentative and hard-fought-for expressions of religious toleration that arose during the seventeenth century, particularly in Holland, in England, and in the American Colonies.

In American history, Puritan Calvinism left the most important legacy because of how the Puritans combined traditional Calvinist theology with dedicated Calvinist concern to make all life glorify God and the purpose of life. However, a system of theology dating to John Calvin referred to several formative doctrines that were the bedrock of Protestant theology in the Reformed tradition that in turn became virtually synonymous with Calvinism.

Puritanism became a major shaping force in North American Christianity before the mid-eighteenth century. For example, the most prominent American Puritan theologian was Edwards, who combined a Puritan emphasis on divine sovereignty with a willingness to engage with the new questions being raised through the rise of a rational worldview.

In addition to the earlier five Puritan colonies, New Hampshire and Maine followed up later. Puritanism, with its merits on faith and works, was an excellent implement for subduing the rugged wildness that was New England.

> Puritanism was a cutting edge which hewed liberty, democracy, humanitarianism, and universal education out of the black forest of feudal Europe and the American wilderness. Puritan doctrine taught each person to consider himself significant if sinful unit to whom God had given a particular place and duty, and that he must help his fellow

man. Puritanism, therefore, is an American heritage to be grateful for and not to be sneered at because it required everyone to attend divine worship and maintained a strict code of ethics.

By the mid-eighteenth century, most of the colonial people were Protestants who were devoutly committed to their various denominations. Their main concern for the authority of the Bible and their search for truth had been part of life since the early seventeenth century.

In New England particularly, the fires of Puritanism were never to cease; people were attending meetings and listening to sermons or sleeping during them. They kept themselves outwardly holy by observing the Sabbath, and they attempted to observe other commandments, but generally speaking, they were falling away from the forebears' genuine faith.

During the pre-awakening time,

Most of the colonial were Protestants, devoutly committed to their various churches throughout the eighteenth century, their concern for the authority of the Bible and searching truth had been part of protestant life in America ever since the seventeenth century. Their devotion for the God was good example for us to learn from. Between 56 and 80 percent of the colonial population participated actively in the religious life of one or another denomination.

> From the start, New England's ministers preached a covenant of grace in regular sermons and a national covenant in occasional sermons. In the former it was affirmed that sinners are totally dependent upon the divine mercy, in the latter, redeemed sinners were exhorted to do good works in order that their society might flourish and that they might avoid God's judgments. The way in which New

Englanders linked the covenant of grace and the national covenant defined the way in which New England's sense of mission evolved over time ... Because the sermon was the dominant form of communication in colonial New England, its history is in many ways the history of New England. Most New Englanders who lived a full life would have heard seven thousand sermons *"average nearly two hours each"* while at the same time reading very few books and having little recourse to newspapers and other forms of communication that are taken for granted today.

Two Key Persons of the Awakening Era: Edwards and Whitefield

Edwards's and Whitefield's participation in the great spiritual revival was a great blessing to the revival. They were quite different; Edwards was affiliated with the Congregationalists, and Whitefield belonged to the Anglicans. Others important figures include Gilbert Tennent, affiliated with the Presbyterians; Joseph Bellamy in rural Connecticut; and Samuel Davis in Virginia. They all helped spread the Great Awakening. Whitefield alone went everywhere. They knew what they were after, and they enlisted affective rhetoric to preach about transforming human depravity by the magnificence of divine grace.

During the first half of the eighteenth century, the churches in the thirteen colonies were also transformed. In fact, throughout the two centuries of our national history, all sorts of relations between religious bodies or individuals and civil authorities developed. For example, starting from Rhode Island, the churches' clergies' salaries came from the churches' public tax payments.

From the sociological point of view, the factors behind every religious movement included political and economic factors, the migration of populations, famine, and religious persecution.

Colonial American churches in the eighteen century experienced a "harvest time" when conversions increased memberships and religious vitality surged. These pioneers we were trying to regenerate the church for the sake of God's mercy; they reasserted the sovereignty of God's divine love in conversion. They preached a holy, higher vision of commitment from the church, transferring from churches across the colony.

Among all the elements that contributed to the awakening, the dedication of many preachers' unwavering participation was doubtless the catalyst. Once the little fire was set, coals were added and the spiritual bonfire took off.

In the 1730s and 1740s, there was an unprecedented Great Awakening that Edwards declared "a surprising work of God." Itinerants such as Whitefield and Gilbert Tennent preached to thousands by crossing parish boundaries and denominational labels. As the spiritual movement spread, many religious leaders condemned their enthusiasm and the damage they were causing to ecclesiastical authority.

Year	White Population	No. of Churches in Eight Denominations[a]	Ratio of Churches to Population[b]	Percent Church Adherents to Population at 80 Families per Church
1700	23,071	373	1/598	80
1720	397,346	646	1/615	78
1740	755,539	1176	1/642	74.7
1750	934,340	1462	1/639	75.1
1765	1,478,037	2110	1/700	69
1780	2,204,949	2731	1/807	59

Table 1: Proportion of Church Members in the Populations of the Thirteen Colonies 1700–1785

[a] Eight denominations are represented: Anglican, Baptist, Congregational, Lutheran, Presbyterian, Dutch Reformed, German Reformed, and Catholic.

[b] The number of churchgoers assumes eighty families of six members each per church.

Source: Patricia U. Bonomi and Peter R. Eisenstadt, "Church Adherence in the Eighteenth-Century British Colonies," William and Mary Quarterly 39 (1982), 274.

The dawn of the awakening was blessed with the birth of Edwards, a genius who made history by his mastering many academic areas; this included Locke's philosophy and Newton's discoveries in science and in Christian theology.

Edwards's contribution to theology redirected humanity's true relationship with God in an affirmative way and earned him the undisputed status of the best theologian the United States. He worked tirelessly to help people unify his center of revival theology to the glory of God and to appreciate the supernatural grace and beauty of God.

The Major Denominations at the Dawn of the Awakening Era

The roots of revival began with Theodore Frelinghuysen, a Dutch Pietist, and it later spread to the Scottish-Irish Presbyterians under the ministry of Gilbert Tennent, whose father, William Tennent Sr. (1673–1745), a man of Puritan convictions, had trained three of his four sons and founded the famous Log College, which later became Princeton University.

Gilbert Tennent (1703–1764) adopted the revivalist approach, and as Presbyterian pastor at New Brunswick, he became the central figure in the awakening movement in his denomination. Gilbert was one of few itinerants who followed Whitefield in his journeys; he undertook his own preaching tour of New England at Whitefield's encouragement.

The revival fire spread to the Baptists of Pennsylvania and Virginia before the extraordinary awakening that began in Northampton under the ministry of Edwards in December 1734.

Anglican Church

The church body grew substantially from 1700 to 1750 because of two British missionary organizations, the Society for the Promotion of Christian Knowledge (SPCK), and the Society for the Propagation of the Gospel in Foreign Parts (SPG).

The SPCK (founded in 1698) shipped Americans more than 100 libraries with at least 100 books each. And with the similar efforts, the APG (founded in 1701) financed ministers to evangelize dissenters. By 1730, it had fifty-eight missionaries preaching in every colony but Virginia and Maryland, and by 1776, it had sent at least 329 missionaries to the thirteen colonies.

By the end of 1750, it was estimated that 289 Anglican parishes were among the total; there were 40 percent outside the south as it spread over in every location in the colony compared to 75 percent in 1690.

American Baptist Churches

As one of the many British Anglican Puritans who migrated to North America, Roger William (ca. 1603–1683) arrived in Boston in 1631. He later purchased some land from the Native Americans and founded Providence. William was baptized in 1638, and the first distinct Baptist church in Newport appeared in 1648.

Roger Williams is known for his views on the separation of

church and state, freedom of conscience, and the fair treatment of Native Americans in the acquisition of land by treaties. The great Baptist fellowship of modern times sprung from his early activities in Rhode Island.

The Puritans of the "low Anglican" settlement in Plymouth and Salem started Presbyterianism in New England. During the late seventeenth century, Scottish Presbyterians migrated to the colonies after 1710 because of the economic discrimination fostered by England's trade laws. Their numbers rose from 17,800 in 1640 to 106,000 in 1700. By 1750, about 200,000 Scots had come to America and settled around the New England, New Jersey, and New York areas.

Agitation over the revivals spread among Baptists as well. The older Rhode Island Baptists, stressing the free will of humanity and standing for an educated ministry, were to be found mostly in Rhode Island, Massachusetts, and Connecticut. They were comparatively few in number. Generally speaking, they were suspicious of the excesses of the Great Awakening.

As a result of the revivals, a large number of churches were founded outside the officially recognized, state-established congregations; this was particularly true in New England. These Separatists would allow preaching only by a converted ministry, and they demanded that a congregation be composed only of known saints. This was where the Baptists won new followers. What was more sensible than to limit membership only to those who as adults consciously professed their faith and were baptized? Thus, a large number of Separatist congregations cut themselves off from the state-supported congregational churches and became Baptists.

The Great Awakening was credited to the Baptists, who were very strong prorevivalist and sent out many itinerant lay and clergy preachers to win converts.

The awakening movement started by Baptists from a minor

denominational church turned into one of the country's three major religions by the early nineteenth century. The number of Baptist churches increased by 38 percent during the 1740s, from 96 to 132, and New Light Congregationalists in New England were among the many converts.

Main Puritan Colony of Massachusetts

For the first generation of settlement, it looked as if the New England Puritans would achieve the total reform of life that had excluded them in England. New Haven was founded in 1638, and Hartford followed. In 1662, a new charter from England added New Haven to Connecticut. This New England Way set a standard for other Puritan settlements.

In the view of the Puritans, the covenant of grace qualified a person for church membership and a voting role in the colony's public life. They also believed the church covenant linked converted individuals to their social relationships.

The churches by and large flourished. This was due to the colony's laws that provided for all individuals to join a church. At the heart of the Puritan experiment in New England were the weekly gatherings in church for worship, fellowship, and instruction. The focal point of Puritan worship was the sermon, the instructional words of God. Their sermons consisted of two parts—the regular (preached twice on Sundays) and occasional (preached at the first meeting each year of the legislatures and on special days of fasting or thanksgiving).

Topics of Preaching and the Spiritual Revivals
A Brief Theology of Preaching Structure

Professor David Buttrick summarized the preaching structure from his homiletic into five key points.

1. Our preaching, commissioned by the resurrection, is a continuation of the preaching of Jesus Christ.
2. In our preaching, Christ continues to speak to the church and through the church to the world.
3. The purpose of preaching is the purpose of God in Christ, namely the reconciliation of the world.
4. Preaching evokes response: the response to preaching is a response to Christ and is properly faith and repentance.
5. Preaching is the Word of God in that it participates in God's purpose, was initiated by Christ, and is supported by the Spirit with community in the world.

The Authority of Preaching

Preaching has been defined in relation to Christ or Scripture; a preacher's personal relationship plays a key factor in his sermons. While if, in a Barthian scheme, Scripture is understood as a God-ordained witness to the Word of God, Jesus Christ, preaching is regarded as a witness to Scripture and a reiteration of the Word of God.

The apostle Paul's rereading of authority is a reminder that preaching is a form of publicly proclaiming the gospel of Jesus Christ's crucifixion and resurrection. Preachers preach in remembrance of Christ's crucifixion in the midst of a saved community. It is a public form of the articulation of Christian faith consciousness.

Summary of Chapter 1

The apostle John gave all believers an infallible declaration of the divine purpose of our Savior's purpose in the world: "We have seen and do testify that the Father sent the Son to be the Savior of the World" (1 John 4:14).

The true meaning of the Great Commission is about believers' obedience to God. Jesus took on the form of man and set the example of obedience in receiving the baptism by the apostle John to fulfill all righteousness.

In 2 Corinthians 3:17, we read, "Now the Lord is the Spirit; and where the Spirit of the Lord is, there is liberty." Only the Spirit of God can lift the veil (law) and help us see the holy mirror of Christ. And where the Spirit goes, the truth is made manifest. The truth will set us free.

As evangelists such as Edwards and Whitefield were beholding Him by just looking at Christ, they stayed in the Word of God and were faithful to the Lord. They had the assurance of the Holy Spirit in the words they were preaching.

Two major factors at the dawn of Great Awakening contributed to religious liberty.

First, religious toleration began after the second group of colonies was founded in Rhode Island in 1660. This allowed limited dissenting sects among colonies to enjoy much more worship.

As for the rest of the regions of New England, the Baptists, Quakers, and Anglicans were still struggling to contribute to the existing Congregational church. By the mid-eighteenth century and before the awakening, the Church of England was still forcing Virginia dissenters to pay taxes to the Anglican Church, which had a monopoly on issuing marriage licenses.

During the awakening era, the common dissenters in almost every colony had made great gains economically and in civil liberties that had prepared the soil for receiving the seeds for gospel.

> The evolution of evangelicalism in America, its emergence as one of the most influential religious and social movements in American history, has produced some specialized characteristics that set it apart from mainstream American Protestantism.

Revivalism

> Revivalism had proved before to be a powerful instrument for healing differences and solving critical social and moral problems. We have to ask ourselves "Could revivalism rise to the challenges posed in the United States in the 1850?"

Evangelists such as Edwards and Whitefield gave their lives to testifying about their faith by openly proclaiming the good tidings of salvation of Jesus Christ. They had one simple purpose for their ministry: to honor God and love their fellow brothers and sisters who didn't know the Lord.

The ministries of Edwards and Whitefield demonstrated that they were true followers of Christ, who reached out to the sheep without the shepherd.

Chapter 2

FRIENDSHIP BETWEEN THE WESLEY BROTHERS AND WHITEFIELD

Whitefield (1714–1770), a Calvinist, evangelist, and revivalist, was born in Gloucester. His parents owned a tavern, the Bell Inn, and as a youngster, Whitefield often served the patrons of the inn. His father died when he was two, and his mother remarried Capel Longden, an ironmonger, when George was eight. He enrolled in the St. Mary de Crypt grammar school at age twelve. He enjoyed reading drama and loved acting.

When he was fourteen, his mother left her husband, and George left the Bell Inn, where he was drawing wine for drunkards. He received communion for the first time when he reentered St. Mary de Crypt grammar school at age sixteen.

His mother had a significant influence upon him at an early age. He had a strong determination to be somebody in the cause of Christ. was a direct consequence of his mother's (Elizabeth's) influence. He sought to follow Christ. That would support his claim that his mother's expectations were "often of service to me in exciting my endeavors to make good in his mother's hopes."

It was during Whitefield's time in grammar school that he developed other special talents in elocution, acting, and dialogue memorization. As a result, he was given many leading roles in school plays. Many people were amazed by his striking providence. His dramatic gift and what he learned about movement, gesture, and tone of voice would help him in his open-air ministry.

When Whitefield was seventeen, he was seriously religious and served God to the best of his knowledge. In 1732, he enrolled in Pembroke College at Oxford. He was a servitor (a messenger boy for seniors) to make some money there. About a year later, he became acquainted with Methodism, which he loved as much as he did his own soul.

Wesley's "Holy Club" Impact on Whitefield

John Wesley attended Christ Church College at Oxford. Wesley and a group of friends stayed together to live a holy life. They were called Methodists by their schoolmates.

Wesley was a spiritual giant even with his roots in Enlightenment England, a belief system developed by John Locke and applied by the Whig establishment of the Church of England.

Charles Wesley (1707–1788) was one of the key members of the Holy Club. He was the first one to reach out to Whitefield with warm greetings that eventually touched Whitefield's heart and persuaded him to join the Holy Club.

Whitefield arrived at Pembroke College as a raw, provincial youth with a West Country accent. He came from the taproom of the family inn, where he worked his way through college waiting on richer students. "As for my quality, I was a poor drawer," he wrote.

Whitefield had heard of the Holy Club before he arrived, and under Charles Wesley's kind invitation for breakfast (Charles violated Oxford conventions by inviting Whitefield—a servitor—to breakfast), he was swiftly drawn to the fellowship. Open hearted and emotional Charles, not the steel-willed and self-controlled John, was Whitefield's chief Oxford mentor.

The Holy Club was little known outside the university at that time. It was composed of eight or nine students who met to help one another in their academic work and maintained a strict regime they had set for themselves. When John Wesley was their moderator, he motivated other members in matters of self-discipline with his strong presence.

Whitefield always treasured his Oxford club's early experience and spoke "with the utmost deference and respect" of the Wesley's brothers, who had been in the famous boarding school and were his seniors. At times of distress for Whitefield during his time at Oxford, he was sent for advice to John Wesley. Thanks to his "excellent advice and Management," Whitefield "was "delivered from the wiles of Satan." It was critical for a youth such as Whitefield to have a subservient relationship. Whitefield wrote, "From time to time Mr. Wesley permitted me to come to him and instructed me as I was able to bear it." Whitefield deferred to John Wesley as his "spiritual father in Christ," and his letters always addressed Wesley as "Honored sir."

Whitefield proved to be an able student in academics, and his concept of the necessity of diligence is manifest in his statement about the practices of others: "It has often grieved my soul to see so many young students spending their substance in extravagant living, and thereby entirely unfitting themselves for the prosecution of their studies."

At Oxford, Whitefield read *The Life of God in the Soul of Men*, a book written by a Scotsman, Henry Scougal. The book cited the miracle of "the new birth," and he assumed that by performing good works, he would place himself on the pathway to heaven. However, this book convinced him that all such assumptions were utterly false.

The discovery helped him with concern, and he wrote that by it, "God showed me that I must be born again, or be damned! I learned that a man may go to church, say prayers, received the sacrament, and yet not be a Christian. God soon showed me, for in reading a few lines further, that "true Christianity is a union of the soul with God, and Christ formed within us." a ray of divine light was instantaneously darted into my soul, and from that moment, and not till then, did I know I must become a new creature.

In 1734, Whitefield embarked on further severe self-disciplinary measures and found his health broken; this affected him all his life.

By age twenty-one, Whitefield was solicited to enter holy orders. Of this, he was greatly afraid, being deeply sensible of his own insufficiency. But the bishop who sent for him told him, "Though I had purposed to ordain none under twenty-three, yet I will ordain you whenever you come." With several other providential circumstance concurring, Whitefield submitted and was ordained on Trinity Sunday 1736.

In 1735, after five years of penitence, Whitefield became the first of the Oxford Methodists to find "a full assurance of faith upon my disconsolate soul." Whitefield began his evangelizing and preaching career.

Whitefield's Conversion

Whitefield's college life, especially the first part of it, brought upon him the criticisms of both friends and foes. George Whitefield wrote about his conversion.

"The recital of his diabolical buffetings is more minute than sensible, and was sure to excite the sarcastic laughter of man like Lavington. The taciturnity that came over him is neither to be desired nor commended." His religious jargon, partly bracketed and partly otherwise, is not "good to the use of edifying. The lengthy descriptions of his fasting, prayers and devotions have a somewhat pharisaic tinge. But, north standing all these animadversions, this section of Whitefield's autobiography is useful and important." While by this time, according to his journal, "Thus employed, I continue in my own city. Three months longer-despised indeed by man, but highly blessed by the grace of God. My understanding was enlightening, my will broken, and my affections more enlivened with a zeal for Christ. Many such, I believe, were added to our little Society as shall be saved."

Since the fall of 1734, Whitefield had been undergoing spiritual strivings and not kept close fellowship with the Holy Club. When Lent was approaching in 1735, for the span of six weeks of his holy season, he determined that he would allow himself little except coarse bread and sage tea without sugar. Whitefield was praying; he had been touched by the Spirit in John 7:37: "Let anyone who is thirsty come to Me." He cried out, "I am thirsty!" and recalled that when Jesus uttered these words, His struggle was almost over. He realized too that for the first time in his life he had implicitly renounced any claim on God's favor and explicitly acknowledged his helplessness. As the moment went by, Whitefield was immediately granted assurance of his new nature in Christ and new standing before God.

> God was pleased to remove the heavy load, to enable me to lay hold of his dear Son by a living faith, and by giving me the Spirit of adoption, to seal me, even to the day of everlasting redemption. O! With what joy-joy unspeakable-even joy that was full of and big with glory, was my soul filled when the weight of sin went off, and an abiding sense of the love of God broke in upon my disconsolate soul! Surely it was a

day to be had in everlasting remembrance. My joys were like a springtide and overflowed the banks. Whitefield testified concerning this experience not long before his death, looking back upon this life-transforming event, he declared, "I know the place: it may be superstitious, perhaps, but whenever I go to Oxford I cannot help but to remember that place where Jesus Christ first revealed himself to me, and gave me new birth."

By that time, Whitefield was convinced that he "must be born again" or outward religion would profit him nothing. He joined the Holy Club in fasting on Wednesdays and Fridays, in visiting the sick and those imprisoned and reading mostly religious books. This was the key period that led him directly to an experimental knowledge of Jesus Christ and Christ's crucifixion.

Preparing for Ordination

Whitefield's self-examination of his spiritual condition was quite serious; he wrote,

> I strictly examined myself by the qualifications required for a minister in St. Paul's Epistle to Timothy, and also by every question that I knew was to be publicly put to me at the time of my ordination.

I can sense that the apostle Paul's spirit spoke to Whitefield in Romans 13:11: "And do this, knowing the time, that now it is high time to awake out of sleep; for now our salvation is nearer than when we first believed." I can relate to the spiritual discernment rooted in the apprehension of divine revelation. Paul's stress on the role of the mind makes it evident it had touched Whitefield's heart.

The Ministry of Whitefield

In his first sermon, Whitefield reported,

> Last Sunday ... I preached my first sermon, in the church of St. Mary de Crypt, where I was baptized ... Curiosity drew a large congregation. The sight at first awed me, but I was comforted with a heartfelt sense of the divine presence and soon found the unspeak able advantage of having been accustomed to speaking when a boy at school, and of exhorting and teaching the prisoners and poor people whilst at the University. By these means, I was kept from being daunted over-much. As I proceeded I perceived the fire kindled, till at last, though so young and amidst a crowd of those who knew me in my infant childish days, I trust I was enabled to speak with some degree of Gospel authority. Some few mocked, but most, for the present, seemed struck, and I have since heard that a complaint has been made to the Bishop that I drove fifteen mad on the first sermon. The worthy Prelate ... wished that the madness might not be forgotten before next Sunday.

> From the very beginning of Whitefield's ministry, several of the aristocracy was present at every service. In reference to this early period of his preaching, one of these titled persons wrote: The preaching of Mr. Whitefield excited an unusual of attention among persons of all ranks. In many of the city churches he proclaimed the glad tidings of great joy to listening multitudes, which were powerfully affected by the fire which was displayed in the animated address of this man of God. Lord and Lady Huntingdon constantly attended wherever

he preached and Lady Anne Frankland became one of the first fruits of his ministry among the nobility.

Partnership: Revival Takes Off

I considered the most important event for Whitefield's career occurred in 1736, when John Wesley entrusted the newly ordained Whitefield with the oversight of the Oxford Methodists while Wesley was away in Georgia. In his journal recorded on his sermon 53, Wesley wrote,

> On Sunday, April 29 1739, Whitefield preached for the first time in *Moorfields*, and on *Kenning ton* Common; and thousands of hearers were as quiet as they could have been in a church. Being again detained in England from month to month, he made a little excursion into several counties, and received the contributions of willing multitudes for an orphan-house in **Georgia**. The embargo which was now laid on the shipping gave him leisure for more journeys to various parts of England, for which many will have reason to bless God to all eternity. At length, on August 14, he embarked: but he did not land in Pennsylvania till October 30. Afterwards he went through Pennsylvania, the Jerseys, New York, Maryland, Virginia, North and South Carolina; preaching to all along to immense congregations, with as great effect as in England. On January 10, 1740, Whitefield arrived at **Savannah**."

John Wesley was an Arminian. What he believed was that God would ensure that all humanity would be saved. Whitefield was a strict Calvinists who subscribed to double predestination. Whitefield accused Wesley of the heresy of universalism and remained Wesley, "Your God is my devil." It was necessary to "rouse the soul out of its carnal security," which Wesley's assurances of salvation induced. But Wesley did not concern himself much with such matters. Right to the end, he thought of himself as an Anglican: "I live and die a member of the Church of England. None who regard my judgment or advice will ever separate from it." The reason that John Wesley was considered Arminian was that he followed Dutch theologian Jacob Arminius, who stressed the completeness of Christ's sacrifice for all people, rejecting John Calvin's view of human depravity and his point about predestination. Wesley was holding a moderate Arminian position; he and Whitefield were reconciled as friends. Wesley graciously preached a sermon of warm commendation at Whitefield's funeral.

The Awakening: Methodist Revival

In the English-speaking churches, the age of reason became the age of renewal. The tide of rationalism was stemmed. Deadening formality was replaced by a fresh wind of the Spirit. This rebirth took place in the 1730s and 1740s. Its roots lay in the Pietism movement in Europe as well as in the lively force of Puritanism. In Britain, the movement was known as the Evangelical or Methodist Revival (interchangeable terms).

In the North American colonies it was called the Great Awakening. It began in Northampton, Massachusetts, under Jonathan Edwards in 1734. This preceded the conversions of both George Whitefield and the brothers John and Charles Wesley, and can be regarded as feeding the Evangelical Revival in Britain. The movement came to fruition in New England between 1740 and 1743, the time of George Whitefield's whirlwind visit.

Whitefield's Open-Air Preaching

We read about Jesus' compassionate outdoor style of preaching described in the gospel accounts of the Sermon on the Mount. It reflected God's love and desire to reach the multitudes without the shepherd.

Biblical examples of outdoor preaching include the prophet Jonah, who after he first disobeyed God's command, eventually went to Nineveh and preached. "And Jonah began to enter the city on the first day's walk. Then he cried out and said, 'yet forty days and Nineveh shall be overthrown.'"

Whitefield devoted his life to preaching. When the churches refused to allow him to use their pulpits, he turned to the outdoors for preaching and averaged twenty sermons a week.

In 1738, Whitefield made the bold move of preaching outdoors first to the grimy coal miners around Bristol and then to the street poor of London. This had turned Methodism outward from respectable Anglican societies toward the masses. Whitefield was on the move to push the reluctant Wesley into following him as a field preacher.

Though Whitefield was considered one of the founders of Methodism [2], the Wesley brothers had laid the foundations of Methodism at Oxford when Whitefield was eighteen. Whitefield followed Wesley's path and later became an enthusiastic evangelist.

The Wesley brothers accepted the invitation of James Oglethorpe to minister to the Native Americans in the colony of Georgia in 1735; they spent two disappointing years there. Whitefield followed John Wesley to Georgia and was appointed minister in Savannah. During this time, Whitefield began reading prayers twice a day and visited the sick daily.

Whitefield was fully committed to the Lord during his days in Georgia. On Sundays, he expounded at five in the morning, read prayers at ten, and preached at three in the afternoon. At seven in

---

[2] Houghton Mifflin Harcourt, the Riverside Dictionary of Biography, 2004.

the evening, he expounded on church catechism.

Whitefield returned to England in 1739 to be admitted to priests' orders. The Wesleys and Whitefield worked closely as brothers as Whitefield won converts with his amazing oratory. He relied on John Wesley's talent to be in charge of organizing events and instructing converts.

Whitefield Answered the Call for Outdoor Preaching

Whitefield had the ability to attract the common people in England at the beginning of his career. Despite the fact that common people thronged to hear him, church authorities took great offense at Whitefield's innovations of preaching the gospel outside church. They were determined to prevent him from preaching in any of their pulpits. What Whitefield had adopted by choice then became a necessity. At the time, the idea of outdoor, extemporaneous preaching with no wooden pulpit or even sermon notes between preacher and congregation seemed to the established church as revolutionary and undignified.

It was at this point in early 1738 that Whitefield concluded that his calling was to be an itinerant preacher to urban areas throughout the Anglo-American world. It was during his preaching tours of American colonies in 1739 and 1740 that the Great Awakening erupted.

Whitefield's first stop was Philadelphia, a major port city, the most cosmopolitan in the New World; it had a thriving market economy. At every stop along Whitefield's ministry tour from Philadelphia to New York and back, record audiences often exceeded the population of the towns in which he preached.

Discord: Fight over the Issue of Grace

An unfortunate incident happened in early 1740 when Wesley and Whitefield were locked in heated debate regarding the issue of the infant Methodist movement. Whitefield was actively opposed by his fellow churchmen; as parish pulpits were denied him, he started preaching in the open air. They were eventually split irrevocably into two different courses.

> It has long been recognized that there were doctrinal differences between John Wesley and George Whitefield, and the point we have now reached in our narrative is that at which a separation appeared between two men. Since this affair played a highly important part in their lives, we have no choice but to look into it. It has, however, generally been reported in a manner strongly in Wesley's favor, and therefore we must attempt to rectify matters to some extent.

The Wesley's were unshakable Arminians who denied predestination, while Whitefield was influenced by the American Calvinists' theory. Nonetheless, Whitefield wrote to Wesley on Christmas Eve 1740 defending his view of the Calvinist doctrine of grace.

The controversy was fueled as Whitefield was invited to preach in Wesley's headquarters at London Foundry. He scandalized the congregation by preaching "the absolute decrees [of election] in the most offensive manner" while Charles Wesley sat there fuming. The letters reflected a major difference between John Wesley and Whitefield; letters exchanged between the two help us understand their major theological differences.

Letter X between Wesley and Whitefield (Whitefield quoted Grace Issue)

"Do not quench the Spirit" (1 Thessalonians 5:19). According to Wesley's biblical interpretation, "Quench not the Spirit wherever it is, it burns, it flames in holy love, in joy, in prayer, in thanksgiving.

O Quench it not, damps it not in yourself or others, either by neglecting to do good, or by doing evil!"

Wesley went further: "Let your conduct be without covetousness; be content with such things as you have. For He Himself has said, 'I will never leave you nor forsake you.'"

Two Letters Whitefield Wrote to Wesley Dated May 24, 1740

At letterhead, "No, dear Sir, Your Mistake" Whitefield quoted Galatians 2:11: "But when Cephas came to Antioch, I opposed him to his face, because he stood condemned."

> I am very well aware what different effects publishing this letter against Mr. Wesley's sermon will produce. Many of my friends who are strenuous advocated for **universal redemption** will immediately be offended. Many who are zealous on the other side will much rejoice. They were lukewarm on both sides and are carried away with carnal reasoning will wish this matter had never been brought under debate. The reasons I have given at here beginning of this letter, I think are sufficient enough to satisfy all of my conduct herein. I desire therefore that they who hold election would not triumph, or make a party on one hand (for I detest any such thing) - and that they who are prejudiced against that doctrine be not too much concerned or offended on the other. Known unto God is all his ways from the beginning of the world. The great day will discovery why the Lord permits Dear Mr. Wesley and me to be of a different way of thinking. At present I shall make no enquiry into that matter, beyond the account which he has given of it in the following letter, which I lately received from his own hands.

Based on this, Whitefield clearly opposed Wesley's stand on universal redemption. Whitefield wrote,

> By then, honored Sir, I cannot but think you have been much mistaken in imagining that your tempting God, by casting a lot in the manner you did could lay you under an *indispensable obligation* to any action, much less to publish your sermon against the doctrine of **"predestination to life."**

Wesley's Reply to Whitefield

> London, August 9, 1740
>
> My Dear Brother,
>
> I thank you for yours, May the 24th, the case is quite plain. There are bigots both for predestination and against it. God is sending a message to those in either side. But neither will receive it, unless from one who is of their own opinion. Therefore, for a time you are suffered to be of one opinion, and I of another, but when his time is come, God will do what man cannot, namely, make us both of one mind. Then persecution will flame out, and it will be seen whether we count our lives dear unto ourselves, so that we may finish our course with joy. I am, my dearest brother,
>
> Ever Yours,
>
> J. Wesley
>
> Thus my honored friend, I heartily pray to hasten the time, for his being clearly enlightened into all the doctrines of divine revelation, that we may thus

> being closely united in principle and judgment as well as heart and affection. And then if the Lord should call us to it; I care not if I go with him to prison like Paul and Silas, I hope we shall sing praise to God, and count it our highest nor to death for honor to suffer for Christ's sake, and to lay down our lives for the brethren.

Whitefield mentioned later even further painfully in his second letter, dated December 24, 1740,

> For some time before, and specially since my last departure from England, both in public and private, by preaching and printing, you have being promoting the doctrine of universal redemption. And when I remember how **Paul** reported **Peter** for his dissimulation, *I fear I have been sinfully silent too long.*
>
> O then don't be angry with me, dear and honor Sir, if now I deliver my soul, by telling you that I think in this you greatly err. I shall only make a few remarks upon your sermon, entitled **"Free Grace."** And before I enter upon the discourse itself, give me leave to take a little notice of what in your *Preface* you term an indispensable obligation to make it public to the whole world, I must own, that I always thought you were *quite mistaken upon that head.*

Devout Whitefield Worked Right after His Wedding

On November 14, 1741, Whitefield, age twenty-seven, married Elizabeth Burnell, a widow age thirty-six. He apparently did not allow the marriage to interrupt his commitment to evangelistic preaching since he was not home when his wife gave birth to their first child.

Whitefield returned to Georgia and made extensive preaching tours. In 1741, the major differences on predestination led to his separation as a rigid Calvinist from John Wesley as an Arminian.

Whitefield's supporters built him a chapel in Bristol and the Moorfields Tabernacle in London. Many of his adherents followed the Countess of Huntingdon in Wales and formed Calvinistic Methodists; she appointed him her chaplain and built and endowed many chapels for him.

Their friendship continued though the old wound was not forgotten. Writing his *A Short History of Methodism* in 1765, John Wesley did not conceal his conviction that Whitefield's view of Calvinism had made "the first breach" in the revival.

Whitefield began his venture as a missionary from England to the new colony of Georgia, where he worked and had a great desire to finance a school for orphans. As he began his preaching tour in 1739, the Great Awakening was already underway in Massachusetts and Connecticut.

Whitefield also made preaching tours from Georgia to Maine in 1740. Later in 1740, his tour attracted followers from all different backgrounds—from clergymen to the general public. In Philadelphia, Whitefield was greeted by crowds of 6,000 and 10,000 at two gatherings.

Whitefield wrote in his journal (November 9, 1749, in Philadelphia),

> Several came to see me and I prayed with them. I preached at eleven in the morning, to several thousands in a house built for that purpose since my departure from Philadelphia. It is a hundred feet long and seventy feet broad. Both in the morning and the evening, God's glory filled the house … Great was the joy of most of the hearers when they saw me; but some still mocked. Between services … many

friends being in the room, I kneeled down, prayed and exhorted them all. I was greatly rejoiced to look around then, because there were some who been marvelous offenders against God. I shall mention two only.

The first is a Mr. Brockden, recorder of deeds, etc., a man eminent in his profession, but for many days a notorious Deist. In his younger days, he told me, he had some religious impressions, but coming into business, the cares of the world so chocked the good seed, that he not only forget his God, but at length began to doubt of, and to dispute His very Being ... When I came to Philadelphia this time twelve-month, he had no curiosity to hear me. But a brother Deist, his choicest companion, pressing him to come to hear me, to satisfy his curiosity he at length complied with his request. It was night. I was preaching at the Court House stairs, upon the conference which our Lord had with Nicodemus. I had not spoken much before God struck his heart ... His family did not know he had come to hear me. After he came home, his wife, who had been at the sermon, came in also, and wished heartily that he had heard me. He said nothing. After this another of his family came in, repeating the same wish; and, if I mistake not, after that another, till at last being unable to refrain any longer, with tears in his eyes, he told them that he had been hearing me ... Though upwards of threescore years old, he is now, I believe, born again of God.

To other is Captain H–I, formerly as great a reprobate as I have ever heard of, almost a scandal and reproach to human nature ... By God's grace, he is now, I believe a Christian. Not only reformed but renewed. The effectual stroke, he told me, was given when I preached last spring at Pennytack ... Ever since, he has been zealous for the truth, stood firm when he was beaten, and in danger of being murdered some time ago by many of my opposers, and in short shows forth his faith by his works. I mentioned these cases in particular, because I think they are remarkable proofs of the doctrine of God's eternal election and everlasting love. Whatever man's reasoning may suggest, if the children of God fairly examine their own experience-if they do God justice, they must acknowledge that they did not choose God, but that God chose them.

Whitefield's preaching tour generated enormous enthusiasm across the colonies.

Not until the Englishman Whitefield's spectacular American tour were those diverse local movement knit together into a larger inter-colonial revival. A particularly vivid account of one stop on Whitefield's journey has been left to us by a Connecticut farmer named Nathan Cole, whose rather ordinary life was transformed by Whitefield's appearance, let us attend first to the sounds and images Cole uses to describe the day that the itinerant first arrived in his vicinity. Now it pleased God to send Mr. Whitefield into this land; and my hearing of his preaching at Philadelphia, like one of the old apostles, and many thousands flocking to hear him preach the gospel, and great numbers were converted to Christ, I felt the Spirit of God drawing me by conviction; I longed to see and hear him and wished he would come this way … Then on a sudden in the morning about 8 or 9 of the clock there were peoples notified by a messenger who informed them that Mr. Whitefield preached at Hartford. The news was spread out quickly that Whitefield had preached a day earlier and is to preach at Middletown this morning at ten of the clock. I was in my field at work. I dropped my tool that I had in my hand and ran home to my wife, telling her to make ready quickly to go and hear Mr. Whitefield preach at Middletown, then ran to my pasture for my horse with all my might, fearing that I should be too late. Having my horse, I with my wife soon mounted the horse and went forward as fast as I thought the horse could bear; and when my horse got much of breach, I would get down and put my wife on the saddle and bid her ride as fast as she could and not stop or slack for my except I bade her, and so I would run until several times to favor my horse … [A]s I drew nearer, it seemed like a steady stream of horses and their riders, scarcely a horse more than his length behind another, all of a latter and foam wit sweat, their breath rolling out of their nostrils every jump. Every horse seemed to go with all his might to carry his rider to hear news from heaven for the saving of souls … [A]all along the 12 miles I saw no man at work in his field, but all seemed to be gone.'"

Theology of the Great Awakening

Especially during the awakening era, it was difficult to be theologically consistent. Early revivalists such as Tennent, a Presbyterian, preached a famous sermon titled "The Danger of an Unconverted Ministry" (1740) in which he urged listeners to reject unconverted ministers.

Rev. Tennent urged congregations to follow other preachers, including itinerants. But George Whitefield and Jonathan Edwards rejected such views, and Tennent soon changed his own mind. By 1742, Tennent, like Edwards, had come to view itinerant and lay preaching alike with suspicion. He thundered that "ignorant young converts" who preached introduced "the greatest errors and the greatest anarchy and confusion.

What may be the most famous controversy involved Gilbert Tennent, who, in the town of Nottingham along the Maryland-Pennsylvania border in the winter of 1740, preached his most famous, or notorious, *The Danger of an Unconverted Ministry.*

He used the story of the Pharisees to imply a condemnation of the opponents of the revival as unconverted and worldly men more interested in maintaining their own privileged positions in the church than in spreading the Gospel or ministering to the needs of their hearer. "All the Doings of unconverted Men." he said, "not proceeding from the principles of Faith, Love, and a new Nature ... but flowing from, and tending to Self, as their Principle and End; are doubtless damnably Wicked and do deserve the wrath and curse of a Sin-avenging God." It was the hearers' duty to shun such persons and seek out ministers who gave direct evidence of personal conversion, more than any other revivalist sermon, *The Danger of an Unconverted Ministry* stood out for the **Old** side as symbol of everything that was wrong with the revival.

Calvinism's predestination theology still dominated New England revivals and the Dutch reformed revivals in New Jersey in the early 1720s. The writings of Edwards had contributed to Calvinism's revival in the eighteenth century as it even bore the New England theology label.

> Theological diversity also characterized the revivals. Calvinists still believing in predestination dominated the New England revivals. The Dutch Reformed revivals in New Jersey in the 1720s stemmed from pietistic influence from Germany. The Presbyterian revivals in the middle colonies were strongly affected by the charismatic leadership of that denomination's ministers Gilbert, John, and William Tennent. They intimated that they bore special signs of divine favor or even supernatural possession.

Tennent described how his brother William had once been raised from the dead, and John Tennent was known for his frequent flights of ecstatic, mystical religiosity: "He often took the Bible in his hand, and walked up and down the room, weeping and mourning over it."

New England Protestantism and Theology

The New England protests in the early 1700s were labeled as New England doctrinal, social, and emotional tendencies of what was called the moderate enlightenment of colonial history.

The changing climate of a growing liberalism over the older Calvinism carried the new attitude toward religion that was hence characterized by moderation and the parting from extremes.

Attributed to the shifting of this era in the American colonial religion were the writings of Samuel Clarke, Lord Shaftesbury, and Francis Hutcheson that supplanted the older Puritan theology at Harvard and Yale and gave the spiritual force they needed.

New England Puritanism and Its Impact on Evangelicalism and Revivalism

Breakthroughs in printing's popularity played a big role in the circulation of Bibles; in addition to that, the proliferation of correspondence among the clergy also helped the renewals among the social elites in their efforts across the New England region.

> In New England, the once raging fires of Puritanism were banked. People in general attended "meeting," listened to sermon or slept during them, kept holy (outward, at least) the Sabbath, and attempted to observe the other commandments; but they were falling away from the antique faith. Some were simply going through the recognized motions of piety. Others were becoming what were vaguely called Arminian, believing that only good works and a free catholic spirit were necessary for salvation.

Edmund Burke (1729–1792), an Irish statesman and philosopher, moved to England and made an interesting remark regarding the colonies.

> All *Protestantism*, even the most cold and passive, is a sort of dissent, but the religion most prevalent in our northern colonies is a refinement on the principle of resistance: it is the dissidence of dissent, and the Protestantism of the Protestant Region.

The new branch of the colonial Protestant Reformation tree

emphasized the laity. The emerging numbers of the priesthood of believers had changed the traditional colonial church.

The main reason was the increased numbers of private and independent landowners. This change of social status soon swept quickly from Virginia to New England. The new attitude and process carried from church members of Virginia caused lay vestries to gain effective control by neglecting to present the clergy to the governor for permanent induction into office. These social changes brought out complaints from the archbishop of Canterbury, who had the right to hire and fire them as if they were domestic servants.

Local Autonomy

The Anglican laity had gained powers in local vestries; there was vigorous opposition to their attempt to establish an episcopate in America. A similar approach occurred while the Congregational church and the Presbyterians also began.

The Breakdown of the Parish System

A system of parishes started in Virginia and ended up in New England; it was designed to embrace entire communities. With the small population spread over a wide area, it was very difficult to keep close contact with even one parishioner, and regular worship services became impossible.

In New England, the pattern of settlements in small landholdings was to hold meetings at a village center. This was a more effective parish system than the Virginia system.

As the economy and population progressed in the eighteenth century, the religious diversity present from the beginning compromised any attempt to establish a system that presumed the whole community would be under a single church. However, the New England church pattern evolved with the complexity of population diversity that came with the problem. In terms of maintaining the minimum qualifications for church membership, the problem became more acute.

> In an effort to preserve the parish concept, a form of "birthright" was adopted and by this means the collapse of the parish system in New England was deferred until the increase of dissent made its defense a hopeless cause. A full century before disestablishment stripped away the lingering traces of the parish structure in New England, Jonathan Edwards had recognized that these days were numbered and had called upon his fellow Congregationalists to return to their initial emphasis upon the church as a covenanted community of convinced believers.
>
> The New England story was somewhat more complex, for in New England the attempt was made to preserve "gathered" churches within a parish structure. This posed no great problem during the early years when the total population was largely a "sifted" people. But when the children of believers were unable to exhibit the minimum qualifications for church memberships, the problem became acute.
>
> Edwards was a Congregational church pastor, "yet Edwards was willing 'to be called a *Calvinist*, for distinction's sake,' and his thought was pervaded by the same visions that had caught the imagination of both Calvin and the Puritans: the sovereignty and freedom of God; the drama of history as the story both of man's frailty and unworthiness in

comparison with the justice and mercy of a majestic God; the personal and social value of a disciplined, 'holy' life of 'practice.'"

It was the "Diary," "Resolutions," and "Personal Narrative" of Edwards that provided much information about the path of Edwards's spirituality.

Edwards's writings expressed his great spiritual strength as a young man's pursuit of his religious experience. Edwards recalled that at age seventeen, he already had a profound religious experience in which there came into my mind so sweet a sense of the glorious majesty and grace of God that I know not how to express. I seemed to see them both in a sweet conjunction; majesty and meekness; a high, and great, and holy greatness.

Edwards's father, Timothy Edwards, had a personal collection of books that included many Puritan authors such as Richard Baxter, John Norton, Samuel Willard, and William Williams. Under his father's influence, Edwards recalled that at very young age, he had a sense of the divine that would often kindle up as it were a sweet burning in his heart, an ardor of soul that he did not know how to express. Edwards wrote,

> Not long after I first began to experience these things, I gave an account to my father of some things that had passed in my mind. I was pretty much affected by the discourse we had together; and when the discourse was ended, I walked abroad alone, in a solitary place in my father's pasture, for contemplation. And as I was walking there and looking upon the sky and clouds, there came into my mind so sweet a sense of the glorious *majesty*

and *grace* of God, as I know not how to express.—I seemed to see them both in sweet conjunction; majesty and meekness joined together: it was a <u>sweet</u>, and <u>gentle</u>, and <u>holy majesty</u>; and also a <u>majestic meekness</u>; an awful <u>sweetness</u>; a high, and great, and <u>holy gentleness</u>. I remember the thoughts I used to have of holiness; and said sometimes to myself, "I do certainly know that I love holiness, such as the gospel prescribes." It appeared to me, that there was nothing in it but what was ravishingly lovely; the highest beauty and amiableness-a divine beauty; far purer than anything here upon earth; and that everything else was like mire and defilement, in comparison of it.

Edwards's Views of Grace and Spirit

From Edwards's personal experience, the Spirit works as the "common illuminations and common affections." It will assist the believers' faculties' natural conviction of their sins. What Edwards meant was that only the essence of that Spirit's activity in the saints made it possible for God's saving grace. Edwards summarized God's beauty in his own words.

> God is beautiful; he is, in fact, the ultimate standard of all beauty. Whatever is beautiful is because it is like Him. All beauty has order and unity. When we see Him as He is, we will behold beauty-ultimate, infinite, and unadulterated beauty-as it truly is.

The seeds of the Awakening were sown in 1734 when Jonathan Edwards began to preach revivalist sermons at Northampton, Mass. This man, pure and simple in his life, was an original thinker in the realms of theology and philosophy. In another environment he might have acquired the fame of George Berkeley, whose idealistic philosophy he anticipated at the age of fifteen; or of John Locke, whose *Essay on Human Understanding* he read in his sophomore year at Yale, with far higher pleasure, he said, "than the most greedy miser finds when gathering up handfuls of silver and gold from some newly discovered treasure." Equally remarkable are his boyhood notes on the habits of the flying spider, praised for their accuracy by leading entomologists of today; and his account of his conversion at the age of seventeen, one of the most beautiful records of that Christian phenomenon since St. Augustine.

The main doctrinal work was the careful and strict inquiry into modern prevailing notions of free will; if God determines everything, how can people have free will?

Borrowing from *John Locke's Essay*, Edwards believed that as long as one had the power to choose and one was free to act independently, each person who acts freely is responsible for his or her acts, so merits are rewarded as well as punishment and blame. We can rest content with the definitions of Locke and Edwards, who both regarded choice as the characteristic of will.

> That conclusion led Edwards to the Original Sin and its problem of imputation of Adam's sin, a problem he solves through the philosophical notion of identity and his theory of continued creation. That God created the first man as the first of men implies that Adam and his nature prior to his apostasy and his guilt implies that the same order obtains in the children of Adam, that sharing his nature, they follow the steps of his fall. But God not only

creates being: he preserves and upholds it in times. Hence, the first creation differs from the last "only circumstantially," and the first apostasy from the last not at all.

Edwards was a theologian: "Edwards in appealing for new birth than were American theologians in defending the broadly Calvinistic themes so central to his concern."

Edwards's remarks on *The Concept of Spirit* in 1723 mentioned,

> One of the highest excellences is "Love". As nothing else has a proper being but *Spirit*, and as bodies are but the shadow of being, therefore, the consent of bodies to one another, and the harmony that is among them, is but shadow of excellence, therefore, must be the consent of Spirits one to another. But the consent of spirits consists half in their mutual love one to another, and the sweet harmony between the various parts of the universe is only an image of mutual love … The pleasure of the senses, where harmony is not the object of judgment, are the result of equality.

Major Themes of Edwards's Theology

Edwards was a deep Christian thinker who followed Augustine and Martin Luther based on the similar, traditional Protestant theology. Edwards built on Augustine's concept that taught that the autonomous reasoning individual could be saved or improved by God's grace to God's glory. In his *A History of the Work of Redemption*, Edwards wrote,

> First, I would consider Christ's taking upon himself our nature to put him in a capacity to purchase redemption for us. This was absolutely necessary, for

though Christ, as God, was infinitely sufficient for the work, yet to his being in an immediate capacity for it, it was needful that he should not only be God, but man. If Christ had remained only in the divine nature, he could not have purchased our salvation; not from any imperfection of the divine nature, but by reason of its absolute and infinite perfection; for Christ, merely as God, was not capable of either obeying or suffering.

The Major Parts of Edwards's A History of the Work of Redemption

Universal Depravity of Humankind

All humanity shared in the original sin of Adam whereby a supernatural gift of grace was lost. The identity of humankind with Adam was constituted by divine decree, and with the fall, humanity was condemned to lives of sin.

Freedom of Will

The central issue of Edwards's theology was the problem of free will: if God determines everything, how can people have free will? "Free will is a matter of semantics, for the will is free only to choose sin" [3].

Edwards insisted that as long as one had the power to choose and in choosing to act, one is free. Consequently, the person who acts freely is responsible for those acts and so merits praise or blame accordingly. As Edwards stated in his *Freedom of the Will*,

> Not only is it true, that it is easy for a man to do the thing if he will, but the very willing is the doing;

---

[3] Mircea Eliade, Encyclopedia of Religion, 2nd edition, 2700.

> when once he has willed, the thing is performed; and nothing else remains to be done. The willing in practice is the performance of the act willed. For 'tis known that these commanding acts of the will are not one way, and the actions of the bodily organs another: for the unalterable law of nature is, that they should be united, so long as soul and body are united, and the organs are not so destroyed as to be incapable of those motions that the soul commands.

Contrasting with his theology of free will, Edwards had a very interesting post-reformation view on God's jealousy.

> Those who come to Christ need not be afraid of God's wrath for their sins; for God's honor will not suffer by their escaping punishment and being made happy. The wounded soul is sensible that he has affronted the majesty of God, and looks upon God as a vindicator of his honor; as a jealous God that will not be mocked, an infinitely great God that will not bear to be affronted, that will not suffer his authority and majesty to be trampled on, that will not bear that his kindness should be abused. For we see that when men come to be under convictions, and to be made sensible that God is not as they have heretofore imagined, but that he is such a jealous, sin-hating God, and whose wrath against sin is so dreadful, they are much more apt to have sensible exercises of enmity against him than before.

The Legitimacy of the Affections in True Religion

> Edwards believed that faith necessarily involves both the intellect or understanding and the volition

or will. It is an act of affective knowledge, a sense of the heart. Belief inclines the heart toward what the understanding chooses. This holistic approach to religious experience was the linchpin for Edwards's case against both the rationalists and the enthusiasts. Against the former he held that, contrary to their belief, the emotions are legitimate in the religious life. Although he shared with John Locke a fear of the passions, he was unwilling to rule out the affections because he had invested with great care specific cases of emotional religion and found them to be genuine. At the same time, he charged the enthusiasts with ignoring the role of the intellect in religious experience.

Edwards's two most famous writings are *Freedom of Will* (1754) and *Original Sin* (1758). The topic of *Free Will* is that God's will is the utmost best thought over our thought, yet who are we, the created by the almighty God, to dare challenge the Creator regarding the best welfare or interest of humankind? "As Edwards argues in *Freedom of Will* (1754), 'the will always is as the greatest apparent good.' Original Sin traces the root of evil inclination to its origins."

Edwards's "A Treatise Concerning Religious Affections" has been recognized as the best exploration of religious psychology in American literature. This work's central theme was the direct perception of divine things. Part 1 was about the nature of the affections and their importance in religion. Part 2 showed with no certain signs that religions are affections and are truly gracious or not. Part 3 showed the distinguishing signs of truly gracious and holy affections. Edwards pointed out clearly that the greatest of the affections is love; he argued that Christian practice in conformity to Christian rules was the principal sign of true religion.

Whitefield's Roots of Theology

Whitefield was a Calvinist; he broke off with John Wesley because of their differences on theological issues in 1741. All his life, Whitefield was more interested in preaching than theology. He confessed later in a letter to Wesley, "I never read anything Calvin wrote; my doctrines I had from Christ and His apostles: I was taught by them of God." It was this strong sense of divine calling that made Whitefield an effective preacher and a major figure who captured thousands of souls for the Lord.

> John Wesley stands for moderate Arminianism; he and Whitefield were later reconciled though not in their theological views. However, Wesley preached a warm sermon after Whitefield's death.
>
> If Whitefield was the most important preacher of the Great Awakening, Jonathan Edwards was its most important apologist. Questions of revival became the occasion for a string of works that made Edwards America's greatest early theologian and a figure whose work is still the subject of serious academic study and the source of popular theological stimulation.
>
> Luther also lost the support of the humanist, such as *Erasmus*, by 1525. Erasmus had supported Luther's demands for reform at the first but recoiled when he saw that Luther's views would lead to a break with Rome. He also disagreed with Luther's view that man's will was so bound that initiative in salvation must come from God. **Erasmus** emphasized the freedom of human will in his book The Freedom of the Will, which he published in 1524; **Luther** denied freedom of the will in his 1524 book, *The Bondage of the Will*.

THE GREAT AWAKENING

In one of Edwards's early books, *Freedom of the Will* (1754), he presented the traditional Calvinistic points on the nature of humanity and salvation in a powerful new shape. Edwards's basic argument was that the will does not constitute a real entity but is an expression of the strongest motive in a person's character.

As Edwards states in his *Freedom of the Will,*

> Not only is it true, but also it is easy for a man to do the thing if he will, but the very willing is the doing; when once he willed, the thing is performed; and nothing else remains to be done. The willing in practice is the performance of the act willed. For ties known that these commanding acts of the will are not one way, and the actions of the bodily organs another: for the unalterable law of nature is, that they should be united, so long as a soul and body are united, and the organs are not so destroyed as to be incapable of those motions that the soul commands.

Edwards's Theology of Free Will

Edwards categorized the topic of *Freedom of Will* into Moral Agency since Adam had been created in the image of God, the foreknowledge of God as making our doctrine of human action good as in Ephesians 1:3–5.

> Blessed be the God and Father of our Lord Jesus Christ, who has blessed us in Christ with every spiritual blessing in the heavenly places, even as he chose us in him before the foundation of the world, that we should be holy and blameless before him in love he predestined us for adoption as sons through Jesus Christ, according to the purpose of his will.

I ascertain that the phrase explains predestination not simply as a matter of God's decision but as also an act of His love (Hosea 1:1–4).

It has to be a great task to study the theological issue and determine whether we can fully comprehend two issues.

Grounds for Affirming the Divine Prescience

> Edwards proof consists of little more than a citation of texts, declaring future events which depend for their appearance on the voluntary acts of men, or speaking of human agents as implement of Divine purpose,-clay in the potter's hand. It is no doubt that will produce an array of texts that present the other side. But the proof that the Scriptures contain Edwards view is unanswerable; and those who accept his premises cannot stop short of unqualified assertion of the Divine prescience.

Its Relation, if Established, to the Will of Human Agents

> If prescience is proven, will it involve determinism in human action? Foreknowledge of the contingent is not a perfection; and if, rather than have a reign of universal necessity and stereotyped futurity, he willed, in order to prepare scope for a gift of moral freedom, to set up a range of alterative possibilities, he could not render some knowledge conditional for the sake of making any righteousness attainable; leaving enough that is determinate, for science; and enough that is indeterminate, for character.

"There is no absurdity in supposing," wrote Dugald Stewart, "that the Deity may, for wise purposes, have chosen to open a source of contingency in the voluntary actions of his creatures, to which no prescience can possibly extend."

Treatise on the Will: Edwards's Major Publication

In Edwards's famous writing, he held the view that while all human beings have the natural ability to turn to God, they lack moral ability—the inclination—to do so. This determining inclination is the transforming gift of God's grace, though its absence is no excuse for sin. The prolonged debate Edwards confronted continued to the issues he had raised. For example, Edwards was engaging in arguments with the Old Calvinists, followers of the federal or covenant theology. He claimed,

> The will is not a self-determining entity but is the human action which "follows the last dictate of the understanding-"understanding" being taken here "in a large sense, as including the whole faculty of perception or apprehension," the whole "previous disposition" and "motive" of the mind. So the mind's "filial confidence in God," its "spirit of love to God," the understanding of faith which reaches into the depths of human being, is the disposition that "teaches and guides" the man of faith in his behavior.

From 1736 to 1740, Edwards emphasized that perseverance was a key factor condition of justification and a means of assurance: "Not only the first act of faith, But also the after-acts of faith, and perseverance in faith, do justify the sinners."

As Edwards stated in *Freedom of the Will*,

> Not only is it true, that it is easy for a man to do the thing he will, but the very willing is the doing else remains to be done. The willing is the doing; when once he has willed. For 'tis known that these commanding acts of the will are not one way, and the actions of the bodily organs another: for the

unalterable law of nature is, that they should be united, so long as soul and body are united, and the organs are not destroyed as to be incapable of those motions that the soul commands. *Edwards's* refusal to separate internal volition and external performance of the act is germane to his theory of what constitutes religious practice "godly" or "ungodly": "Godliness consists not in a *Heart* to purpose to fulfill God's commandments but in n heart actually to do it." Having a heart or inclination to purpose to perform an act, or being at one remove from the actual performance of the act, is not really to incline to perform it at all. When something is willed, there is an inclination actually to do the act. And the very wiling becomes the doing. It is senseless, therefore, for a man to attempt to excuse his actions by saying that he really willed one thing but did another."

From Northampton to Stockbridge

When Edwards was dismissed by his congregation of Southampton in 1750, he went to Stockbridge, Massachusetts, a frontier Native American village, where for seven years he found contentment pasturing a small church. He ministered to Native Americans mixed with some colonists until 1758. He found leisure to devote his theological and philosophical powers to the defense of Calvinism against Arminianism. During this period, he characterized the liberal theological trends of the eighteenth century.

Though many Edwardians after Edwards were very competent scholars and industrious workers, they unfortunately lacked the poetic insights and breadth of vision their master had long been characterized by.

He upheld a Calvinistic theology and believed that while people have a rational ability to turn to God; because of total depravity they lack the moral ability or inclination. This ability must be imparted by divine grace. He made much of the sovereignty and love of God in his work *Freedom of the will*. He wrote that God's love draws people to Himself and to His service after they have become Christians.

A Contrast of John Wesley and Whitefield

	Wesley	Whitefield
Parentage	Son of an Anglican rector in Epworth	Son of a tavern keeper in Gloucester
Early Life	Strict religious upbringing Raised surrounded by lovely mother, Susanna	Supervised by mother, Susanna influenced by mother, Elizabeth, who was widowed when George was two
Conversion	Alders gate Street, London	Oxford University, at age 21
Ordination	Church of England (1728, at age 25)	Church of England (1736, at age 22)
Preaching Style	Intellectual, doctrinal	Dramatic, emotional
Doctrine	Arminian	Calvinistic
Organizational Style	Exceptional organizer	Not a good organizer; leave organizing to others
Legacy	Methodist	Calvinistic Methodist
Influence on Evangelic	Party in Church of England	Colony of America

The Wesleys laid the foundation for Whitefield's faithful walk of holiness. Whitefield paid that back later by introducing the Wesleys to some of the practices that would characterize their Methodist movement, including preaching outdoors to ordinary people who had been neglected by the established churches.

Whitefield made his seventh and last tour of the American colonies between 1739 and 1770. He had gradually emerged as the key advocate who replaced Edwards.

As the revival continued in New England, it was given a new sense of direction by George Whitefield recently arrived from England. England itself was then experiencing the evangelical revival associated with John and Charles Wesley as well as Whitefield. Edwards found that he was no longer at the forefront of the revival movement. He was also troubled by divisions within his congregation at Northampton, particularly over matters of church discipline. He moved to minister to a congregation at Stockbridge, where relatively light parish duties allowed him to write a series of major theological works that gave intellectual muscle to New England Puritanism.

The arrival of Whitefield in America in 1740 touched off the awakening. He came at the time when revivals were sweeping through the northeastern colonies; thousands experienced the spiritual bonfire of grace even though the Old Lights brought attacks on the revivalists. Edwards, Whitefield, and other evangelical preachers were stirring up religious fanaticism; their efforts and dedication had brought a marked increase in church membership and many invaluable humanitarian undertakings.

Whitefield built on the high tide of the waves of revivals and knitted together disparate revivals in the colonies with his enthusiastic spirit, powerful preaching style, and most of all, the outdoor ministry with which he had reached tens of thousands of hearers across the colonies.

THE GREAT AWAKENING

Appreciation of Whitefield

Whitefield was a very dedicated evangelist. He rode on horseback during most of his itinerant preacher career. It was extremely tough under the conditions of rain or the bitter winter weather and his tight schedules. His efforts, however, were well appreciated wherever he visited. Once an article from The *Pennsylvania Gazette* (July 31, 1746) is below.

> On Sunday the 20th instant, the Rev. Mr. Whitefield prech'd twice, tho' apparently much indisposed, to large Congregations in the New-Building in this City, and the next Day set out for New York. When we seriously consider how incessantly this faithful Servant (not yet 32 Years old) has, for about 10 years past, labored in his great Master's Vineyard, with an Alacrity and fervent Zeal, which an infirm Constitution, still daily declining, cannot abate; and which have triumphed over the most vigorous opposition from whole Armies of invidious Preachers and Pamphleteers; under whose performances, the Pulpits and Presses, of Great Britain and America, have groaned; We may reasonably think with the learned Dr. Watts, "That he is a Man raised up by Providence in an uncommon Way, to awaken a stupid and ungodly World, to a Sense of the important Affairs of Religion and Eternity:" And the Lines of Mr. Wesley, concerning another young Methodist, may Justly be applied to his dear Friend Whitefield— (continued next page)

> Wise in his Prime, he waited not for Noon,
> Convinced that Mortals never lived too soon;
> As if foreboding here his little Stay,

> He makes his Morning bear the Heat of Day.
> No fair Occasion, glides unhealed by,
> Snatching the Golden Moments as they fly,
> He by few fleeting Hours ensures Eternity.

His sermon here this summer have given general Satisfaction, and plainly proved the great ability of the Preacher. His rich Fancy, sound and ripening judgment, and extensive acquaintance with men and books of useful Literature, have been acknowledged by every unprejudiced person. Purity of languages, perspicuity of method, a ready Elocution, an engaging Address, and an apt gesture, peculiar to this accomplished orator, considered with his unspotted character in private life, have added force to the plain strong arguments, and pathetic expostulations, wherewith his discourses abounded. And, it cannot be doubted, that many have been awakened to a Sense of the Importance of Religion, and others have been built up in their most holy Christian Faith under his Ministry."

The Final Day of Whitefield

On September 29, 1770, a Saturday, Whitefield preached his last sermon outdoors. He set out by horseback in the morning from Portsmouth, New Hampshire, to preach at Newburyport, Massachusetts, the next day. On his way, Whitefield galloped nonstop through Exeter, New Hampshire. Many people nearby were aware of his trip and had already gathered in hopes they might hear him preach. They had erected a platform in an outside field and waited for his arrival.

Under the crowd's insistence, Whitefield agreed to speak. When Whitefield approached the platform, an elderly gentleman said, "Sir, you are fit to go to bed than to preach."

"True, sir," Whitefield replied, looking up to heaven. Then he said, "Lord Jesus, I am weary in thy work, but not weary of it. If I have not yet finished my course, let me go and speak for thee once more on the fields, seal thy truth, and come and die."

When Whitefield mounted the platform, he stood for several minutes unable to speak. An observer noted that his spirit was willing but his flesh was dying. Whitefield finally said, "I will wait for the gracious assistance of God, for he will I am certain assist me once more to speak in his name." He then preached for two hours on the verse "Examine yourself whether ye be in the faith."

Toward the end of the message, he said,

> I go; I go to a rest prepared: my sun has given light to many, but now it must set- no, to rise to the zenith of immortal glory. I have outlived many on the earth, but they cannot outlive me in heaven. Many shall outlive me on earth and live when this body is no more, but there-oh, thought divine! I shall be in a world where time, age, sickness, and sorrow are unknown. My body fails, but my spirit expands. How willingly would I live forever to preach Christ? But I die to be with him.

Many of his hearers said that it was the best sermon Whitefield had ever delivered.

Whitefield died on Sunday, September 30, 1770.

Great Preacher

Whitefield's style of delivery was impressive; he memorized sermons and spoke without notes. He changed colonial preaching by varying his voice. He used different gestures—sometimes calm, other times agitated. He seemed to have full control of the listeners' emotions, and he created unique models for preachers to follow; from Charles Finney of awakening time and Billy Sunday in the nineteenth century to Billy Graham of our days.

Despite his detractors, however, Whitefield's undeniable oratorical power, as folk tradition has it, is that he could make an audience laugh or cry by the way he pronounced his words. The word Mesopotamia- brought him large crowds and excited fellow English evangelists. Further, unlike his mentor, Wesley, who based his success on the careful of converts through a hierarchical church organization, Whitefield reveled in preaching to any and all and essentially invented itinerancy as a revival tool. Indeed, with many traditional venues closed to him because of what other clergy perceived as his eccentricity, Whitefield preached often in the open air, an equally radical innovation. By 1737 the editor of the *Virginia Gazette* thought him newsworthy enough to bring him to the attention of an American readership.

Whitefield's major contribution set new and high standards for Christian ministers. His vocal range was excellent; it had benefited from his exposure to drama at an early age. He ranked the highest for his time in drawing huge turnouts—an average of 20,000 to 30,000 wherever he traveled across the colonies. He held his audiences in awe and was the pioneer of American revivalists. Whitefield never left the Anglican Church despite the bitter criticism of his Church of England minister. Other Anglican clergymen treated him as a virtual enemy. But his impact on the awakening movement was enormous.

Whitefield's Theology

Whitefield affirmed the doctrines of predestination, election, and the definite atonement—all themes of traditional Calvinism. He confessed in a letter to Wesley, "I never read anything Calvin wrote. My doctrines were from Christ and His apostles; I was taught them

THE GREAT AWAKENING

by God." This sense of divine purpose made Whitefield an effective preacher and a model to his fellow revivalists. In responding to Wesley's sermon "Free Grace,"

> which he had preached at Bristle in 1740, Whitefield addressed his comments regarding Wesley's sermon (December 1740); Scripture reference of Wesley's sermon "Free Grace": He that spared not his own Son, but delivered him up for us all, How shall he not with him also freely give us all things? (Romans 8:32 King James Version).
>
> How freely does God love the world! While we were yet sinners, "Christ died for the ungodly." While we were "dead in our sins," God "spared not his own Son, but delivered him up for us all." And how freely with him does he "give us all things!" verily, FREE GRACE is all in all! The grace or love of God, whence, cometh our salvation, is FREE FOR All.

It is free in all to whom it is given.

2. The doctrine of predestination is not a doctrine of God.
3. Predestination destroys the comfort of religion, the happiness of Christianity.
4. The uncomfortable doctrine also destroys our zeal for good work.
5. Furthermore, the doctrine of predestination has a direct and manifest tendency to overthrow the whole Christian Revelation.
6. And at the same time, makes that revelation contradict itself.
7. Predestination is a doctrine full of blasphemy.

Whitefield disagreed with the Wesley's faith statements from the sermon. First,

You say that if this be so (i.e., if there is election) then is all preaching in vain: It is needless to them that are elected; for them, whether with preaching or without, will infallibly, therefore the end of preaching is to save souls is void. With regard to them, and it is useless to them likewise. So that our preaching is in vain, and our hearing is also in vain. Second, You say that doctrine of election and reprobation directly tends to destroy Holiness, which is the end of all ordinances of God. For (says the dear Mistaken. Wesley "it wholly takes away that first motive to follow after it, so frequently proposed in Scripture, the hope of future reward, and fear of punishment, the hope of heaven, and the fear of hell, etcetera.

The Domination of Calvinist Theology in the Awakening Era

During the Awakening and in its immediate aftermath, nearly all American evangelicals remained committed to an essential Calvinism. In other words, salvation was wholly the work of God and not of man. That belief distinguished them from such English evangelicals as the Methodist organizer John Wesley, Whitefield's former friend and ally, who combined his message of salvation by faith with the Arminian assertion that it was within the sinner's power to work toward its achievement.

John Wesley's Interpretation of John 3:16

John Wesley's understanding of "believe" from John 3:16 will help us to find his theological stand. Wesley wrote in his notebook what John 3:16 meant to him.

> Yea and this was the very design of God's love in sending him into the world. Whosoever believeth on him-with that faith which work by love, and hold fast the beginning of his confidence stead to the end. God so loves the world-That is, all men under heaven; even those that despise his love, and will for that cause finally perish. Otherwise not to believe would be no sin to them. For what should they believe? Ought they to believe that Christ was given for him? Then he was given for them. He gave his only Son-Truly and seriously. And Son of God gave himself, Galatians 4:4, truly and seriously." Wesley continues with John 3:17–18; "God sent not his son into the world to condemn the world-Although many accuse him of it; He that believeth on him is not condemned-Is acquitted, is justified before the God. The name of only-begotten Son of God-The name of a person is often put for the person himself. But perhaps it is farther intimated in that expression, that the person spoken of is great and magnificent. And therefore it is generally used to express either God the Father or the Son.

The key words of John 3:16 are *believes in*: "that whoever believes in Him should not perish but have everlasting life." We put these two words together in a moral or religious reference used in the New Testament of the conviction and trust to which we are impelled by a certain inner and higher prerogative and law of soul. We are to honor God; He is in charge of the power to give believers the spiritual understanding of trusting Christ's promise to save our souls only with our contrite spirit to believe in Christ and to claim

His promise by living humbly in true spirit. I have nothing to say about the salvation of my soul; it is all unto the Lord!

Summary of Chapter 2

Whitefield, the Anglican cleric and the grand itinerant of the Great Awakening, benefited early in life by developing a great love for the theater. He was befriended by Charles and John Wesley and became a member of their Holy Club. He was one of the founders of Methodism.

He established a reputation as an extraordinary preacher early on. He engaged in his extemporaneous style of preaching with a stentorian voice and dramatic training.

Since Whitefield's conversion in 1735, he was a pioneer of the English revival. After his second visit to colonial America in September 1740, with the blessings from God, Whitefield set off on a six-week, open-air tour that resulted in the most dynamic awakening colonial America had ever experienced.

Christian historians considered Whitefield as a saint of Calvinism, Evangelism, and revivals. His contemporaries described him as the marvel of the age. He was an extremely eloquent preacher who electrified his listeners. He drew unprecedentedly huge crowds wherever he preached. The Great Awakening that swept across the England and North America in the eighteenth century has been attributed mainly to Whitefield's dynamic ministry.

Calvinism is a very ambiguous term.

> used with two quite distinct meanings. First, it refers to the religious ideas of religious bodies (such as the Reformed Church) and individuals (such as Theodore Beza) that were profoundly influenced by John Calvin, or by documents written by him.

Second, it refers to the religious ideas of John Calvin. Although the first sense is by far the more common, there is a growing recognition that the term is misleading." While "Arianism is a major early Christogical heresy, which treated Jesus Christ as the supreme of God's creatures, and denied his divine status. The Arian controversy was of major importance in the development of Christology during the fourth century.

Theological Issues: Calvinism versus Arminianism

	Calvinist Position	Arminian Position
Original sin	Total depravity & guilt inherited	Weakness inherited from Adam
Human will	In bondage to sin	Free to do spiritual good
Grace of God	Common grace given to all	Enabling grace given to all
Saving grace given to select	Saving grace given to those elected	Persevering grace given to those who obey
Predestination	Rooted in God's decrees	Rooted in God's foreknowledge
Atonement	Christ's death a substitution	Christ's death a sacrifice that God penal sacrifice benevolently accepted in place of penalty
Application of	By power of the Holy Spirit	By power of the Holy Spirit in atonement respond to the will of the sinner

Whitefield put all his gifts and talents to good use in preaching the gospel. He gave countless evidence of Jesus' sacrificial love with the orphanage he founded in Georgia. He offered firm testimony of his appreciation for the amazing hand of God on him. He was rejected by the traditional church, but God opened doors for Whitefield to use his theatrical and oratorical talents in outdoor ministry. We have an amazing God; He can do magnificent things to call and train people to evangelize His chosen people. Whitefield is a perfect example of how God's handiwork can serve Him faithfully.

Chapter 3

THE LIFE AND MINISTRY OF JONATHAN EDWARDS

Edwards was born on October 5, 1703, the fifth son of Timothy Edwards, a pastor in East Windsor, Connecticut. Edwards's mother, Ester, was the daughter of Rev. Samuel Stoddart, pastor of Northampton Church, Massachusetts. Samuel Stoddart had great influence on young Edwards.

Edwards was home-schooled by his father. At age sixteen, as a witness to his father's congregation, he wrote *Personal Survival* as captured in his reflection: "Through the wonderful mercy and goodness of God there hath in this church been a very remarkable stirring and pouring out of the Spirit of God."

Edwards's maternal grandfather, Solomon Stoddard, had overseen five "harvests" of souls during his sixty years' ministry. As a young man, he was nurtured and instructed in the reformed theology and followed his parents' strict practices of Puritan piety.

Edwards was admitted to Yale College at age thirteen. He loved philosophy and science and was profoundly influenced by John Locke and Isaac Newton. Edwards wrote papers that covered a variety of topics including spiders, atoms, rainbows, the mind, and being. Edwards graduated in 1720 first in his class.

He was a genius who published many scientific research papers at a very young age at Yale. The reason and purpose of Edwards's study of Newton's new science and Locke's writings was not to become a scientist but to lead a life of holiness.

He was licensed to preach at a Presbyterian church in New York in 1722, where he remained for a short period. After he left, he served as pastor at Bolton, Connecticut.

Edwards continued to study at Yale and became the head tutor of the college in 1724.

Edwards combined an academic rigor that came from his keenness in philosophy with a close attachment to Calvinism that inspired his conversion in 1721.

He was ordained in February 1727. That year, he married Sarah Pierrepont, the daughter of the Congregational minister in New Haven.

Edwards was called by Yale to become assistant pastor to his grandfather Solomon Stoddard in 1726, and he became the sole minister in charge of the Congregational church in Northampton, Massachusetts. In 1729, Edwards became the full-time minister after Stoddard's death.

Edwards's Conversion

It was probably in the spring of 1721 that Edwards was converted. After having been immersed in a reading of 1 Timothy 1:17, Edwards wrote,

> There came into my soul, and was as it were diffused through it, a sense of the glory of the Divine Being; a new sense, quite different from any thing I ever experienced before, never any words of scripture seemed to me as these words did. I thought with myself, how excellent a Being that was, and how

> happy I should be, if I might enjoy that God, and be rapt up to him in Heaven, and be as it were swallowed up in him forever ... From about that time, I began to have a new kind of apprehensions and ideas of Christ, and the work of redemption, and the glorious way of salvation by him. An inward, sweet sense of these things, at times, came into my heart, and my soul was led away in pleasant views and contemplations of them. And my mind was greatly engaged to spend my time in reading and meditation on Christ, on the beauty and Excellency of his person, and the lovely way of salvation by free grace in him.

Scripture was central to his conversion. Edwards also noted the "inward" sweet sense that gripped his soul after his conversion as he meditated upon what Scripture said about God and Christ and on their utterly free and sovereign grace in salvation. As we shall see, such biblical meditation would become central to his piety in *Resolutions* (1722–1723).

Edwards's "Personal Narrative" (Boston 1740), letters, and diaries show that by age seventeen, he had a profound religious experience in which

> there came into my mind so sweet a sense of the glorious majesty and grace of God that I know not how to express. I seemed to see them both in a sweet conjunction; majesty and meekness, a high, and great, and holy gentleness.

> Edwards sought to further the revival spirit at Northampton by preaching against the town's preoccupation with worldly wealth and status, warning God's judgment, and, on a different note,

highlighting the realty of a "divine and supernatural light" that could open one's eyes to God's beauty. Edwards brought to light a powerful and intense preaching ministry, and his sermons are still read today.

Edwards's Spiritual Discipline

As a young man, Jonathan Edwards purposed to order his spiritual life by vowing to live for the glory of God. Such resolve would require him to live with spiritual discipline and a dogged determination in every area of life. Edwards knew that in this pursuit, sin must be forsaken and his tendency to anger resisted. Time must be measured, death must be appraised, and eternity weighed. Life must be lived wholeheartedly, humility must be shown and love practiced. In all this, self must be regularly examined.

Edwards's writings, including his *Resolutions*, were based on the Reformed theology in its English Puritan form. This theology emphasized God's glory and absolute sovereignty and held that Christ was God and was absolutely sovereign.

It is most evident by the works of God, that his understanding and power are infinite; for he that hath made all things out of nothing, and upholds, and governs, and manages all things every moment, in all ages, without growing weary, must be of infinite power. In the person of Christ are conjoined absolute *sovereignty* and perfect *resignation*. This is another unparalleled conjunction. Christ, as he is God, is the absolute sovereign of the world; the sovereign disposer of all events ... [Thus.] the decrees of God are all his sovereign decrees; and the work of creation, and all God's works of providence, are his sovereign works. It is he that worketh all things according to the counsel of his own will. Col. i.16–17: "By him and through him, and to him, are all things." "John v. 17: "The Father worketh hitherto, and I work." Matt. Viii. 3: "I will, be thou clean."

Edwards's Resolutions

Edwards was an extremely disciplined Christian all his life; reading his well-known and respected *Resolutions* gives us an understanding of how much he asked of himself to live a holy life. "Being sensible that I am unable to do anything without God's help, I do humbly entreat him, by his grace, to enable me to keep these Resolutions, so far as they are agreeable to his will, for Christ's sake."

He remembered to read over his resolutions once a week.

Major Contents of Edwards's Resolutions

1. The seventy resolutions include six main headings.
2. Pursuing the Glory of God
3. Forsaking Sin
4. Making Proper Use of God-Allotted Time
5. Living with All His Being for the Lord
6. Pursuing Humility and Love
7. Making Frequent Self-Examination

Edwards, a Calvinist, was well known for his God-centered, God-focused, and God-entranced convictions. Two of the major classic works—*The Westminster Shorter Catechism* (1648) and John Calvin's *Institutes of the Christian Religion* (1559)—had a great impact on his thinking. His Resolutions became a very practical reflection of his daily effort to live in a Reformed theological spirit. Edwards credited his father, Timothy, for teaching him the Shorter Catechism in his childhood.

Edwards dedicated all his life to one main purpose—living a holy life and doing everything for the glory of God.

From Edwards's *Resolutions*, we can trace the influence of Calvin's Institutes on his thinking. The *Institutes* was Calvin's magnum opus, a monumental work that had as its central theme, "May you resolve to live your life not for self but for God." He tried to "Remember to read over his 72 Resolutions once a week" to gauge his personal spiritual progress. This was similar to the Puritans, who were known to submit themselves to divine searching to monitor their personal actions and their motives.

Edwards used a diary to gauge his spiritual growth based on his resolution. For example,

> Monday, December 24. Concluded to observe, at the end of every month, the number of breaches of resolutions, to see whether they increase or diminish, to begin from this day, and to compute from that the weekly account, my monthly increase and out of the whole, my yearly increase, beginning from new-year day.

He even attempted to review his progress in keeping his resolutions while busy with other matters.

> Tuesday morning of June 18. Memorandum: To do this part, which I conveniently can, of my stated exercise, while about other business, such as self-examinations, resolutions, etc. that I may do the remainder in less time.

New England Puritanism

The American colonies had experienced a metaphysical monopoly for nearly two centuries in the philosophical sense ever since the first landing of the Pilgrims, who held the prevalent faith of the colonists and their descendants of the Calvinism of the eighteenth century.

The New England fathers were adhered to by the Puritans across Massachusetts and Connecticut and then later passed through to the Dutch Reformed in New York and New Jersey.

> Thus wide was the influence of Calvinism both as to duration of time and extent of space, for even the Church of England in America contained a large infiltration of Genevan doctrine.

> The very terms Puritan and puritanical conjure images of strangely dressed men and women oppressing American Indians, burning and hanging women wrongly accused of witchcraft, and locking people in stocks for minor infractions of church rules. They are virtually synonyms for moral strictness and religious intolerance. Like all caricatures, these images contain an element of truth, but they do not tell the whole story of Puritanism.

Historians have studied Edwards's role as a pastor and the huge impact his sermons and writings had upon not only the Great Awakening but also on the modern missionary movement.

Edwards was known as the great philosopher of a mystic, traditionally for his character of Puritan divines and the New England conscience. As the key defender of the old faith, Edwards's advocacy of spiritual intuition made the Puritans consider him a saint.

> Edwards is convinced of the verity of mystical intuition. At the same time he is wise enough to state that this may be immediate, it does not come all at once nor arise without painful preparation. There are three stages in the process: First, comes a by great and violent inward struggle the gaining of a spirit to part with all things in the world; then, a kind of vision or certain fixed ideas and images of being alone in the mountains or some solitary wildness far from all mankind; Finally, a thought of being wrapped up in God in heaven, being, as it were, swallowed up in Him forever. In these few words Edwards has summed up the mystic progression presented in the ancient manuals, those three stages in the ladder of perfect, -First, the purgative, brought about by contrition and amendment; Then, the illuminative, produced by concentration of all the faculties upon God; Lastly, the intuitive or unitive, wherein man beholds God face to face and is joined to him in perfect union.

The philosophers labeled Edwards as a mystic because of his marvelous sense of the immediacy of the character with the divine presence. Edwards actually wrote a famous undergraduate paper entitled "Of Being," in which he wrote,

> It follows from hence that those beings which have *knowledge* and *Consciousness* are the Only Proper and Real And substantial beings, inasmuch as the being of other things is only by these. From hence we may see the Gross mistake of those who think material things the most substantial beings and spirits more like a shadow, whereas spirits Only Are Properly Substances.

Edwards's dreadful sermon "Sinners in the Hands of an Angry God" and his famous and rigid treatise on free will eventually led Edwards to be considered a pitiless, professional theologian.

> There is also the positive reason that Edwards gives a definition of the divine language of signs which has been declared truly marvelous as emanating from a mere boy ... Indeed, reasons Edwards, the secret lies here: That, which truly is the Substance of all bodies, is the infinitely exact, and precise, and perfectly stable Idea, in God's mind, together with His stable Will, that the same shall gradually be communicated to us, and to other minds, according to certain fixed and exact established Methods and Laws: or in somewhat different language, the infinitely exact and precise Divine Idea, together with an answerable, perfectly exact, precise, and stable Will, with respect to correspondent communications to Created Minds, and effects on their minds.

Edwards's Roots of Theology

Historians and scholars give more weight to Edwards's writings on philosophical and scientific topics than they do to his contributions to the church and Christian theology.

Earlier tied with John Locke's term "divine and supernatural light," Edwards's effect on human soul was incalculable and irresistible. To him, grace transformed all prior knowledge and affected all actions afterward.

For twenty-three years, Edwards dedicated his time to Puritan orthodoxy and evangelical Christianity as opposed to liberal theology and rational philosophy. Edwards was quite clear about the importance of Jesus' humanity and divinity.

> First, I would consider Christ's taking upon him our nature to put himself in a capacity to purchased redemption for us. This was absolutely necessary, for though Christ, as God, was infinitely sufficient for the work, yet to his being in an immediate capacity for it, it was needful that he should not only be God, but man. If Christ had remained only in the divine nature, he could not have purchased our salvation; not from any imperfection of the divine nature, but by reason of its absolute and infinite perfection; for Christ, merely as God, was not capable of obedience or suffering.

The Controversy of Profession of Faith and Communion

Edwards's ministry succeeded his grandfather's ministry at the Southampton church in Connecticut. His grandfather had issued an open invitation to the communion table, but Edwards adopted a much harder line on the matter; he insisted that new members of the congregation had to make a basic profession of faith before participating in communion. His new rule met resistance from his congregation.

Despite his very successful ministry, Edwards became embroiled in this controversy, which spread into town politics and neighboring ministries. In the end, Edwards was dismissed as minister in 1750. After his removal, in May 1751, Edwards accepted a pastoral call to Stockbridge in western Massachusetts, a mission with few whites and over 250 Native American families. His stayed at Stockbridge and initiated the most productive life there. Edwards continued his study habit and finished several of his major treatises.

In February 1758, Edwards accepted the position of president at Princeton College. After his installation, he began preaching every Sunday in the college chapel. He also taught theology to the senior class and became very popular. A week after his arrival at Princeton, Edwards was inoculated against smallpox; less than a month later, he became a victim of the disease. His condition deteriorated rapidly. He realized he would not see his family again. He wrote to his daughter,

> Dear Lucy, it seems to me to be the will of God that I must shortly leave you; therefore give my kindest love to my dear wife, and tell her, that the uncommon union which has so long subsisted between us, has been of such a nature as I trust is spiritual and therefore will continue forever, and I hope she will be supported under so great a trial, and submit cheerfully to the will of God. And as to my children, you are now to be left fatherless, which I hope will be an inducement to you all to seek a father who will never fail you.

Edwards died on March 22, 1758 and was buried in Princeton's cemetery.

Edwards's Impact on His Peers

Edwards's preaching of a series of revivalist sermons in 1734 rocked church history; he recorded this revival in a pamphlet called *A Faithful of the Surprising Work of God in the Conversion of Many Hundred Souls* in Northampton (1736). He described his parishioners as sober, orderly, and good but lacking in religious fervor.

> But in 1734 two young people died shockingly sudden deaths, and this (backed up, it would appear,

by some fearful words by Edwards himself) plunged the town into a frenzy of religious fervor. People could talk of nothing but religion; they stopped work and spent the whole day reading the Bible. In about six months, there had been about three hundred born-again conversions from all classes of society: sometimes there would be as many as five a week. Edwards saw this craze as the direct work of God himself: he meant this quite literally; it was not a mere *pious facou de parler (truly)*. As he repeatedly said, "God seemed to have gone out of his usual way" of behaving in New England and was moving the people in a marvelous and miraculous manner. It must be said, however, that the Holy Spirit sometimes manifested himself with some rather hysterical symptoms. ... Sometimes, Edwards tell us, they were quite "broken" by the fear of God and "sunk into an abyss, under a sense of guilt that they were ready to think was beyond the mercy of God." This would be succeeded by an equally extreme elation, when they felt suddenly saved. They used "to break forth into laughter, tears often at the same time issuing like a flood, and intermingling a loud weeping. Sometimes they have not been able to forbear crying out with a loud voice, expressing their great admiration. We are clearly far from the calm control that mystics in all the major religious traditions have believed to be the hallmark of true enlightenment.

Edwards's Impact on Wesley and Whitefield

Whitefield read Edwards's *Faithful Narrative* in 1737 at Savannah and began his marvelous career right after that year.

Months later, Wesley also read *Faithful Narrative*. He wrote in his journal of the American revivals, "Surely this is the Lord's doing and it is marvelous in our eyes."

With his leadership in the dual realms of preaching and theology, Edwards helped transmit to younger generations the richer aspect of American Puritanism: the personal experience of spiritual and emotional rebirth.

What Edwards tried to do in the theology of revival was to reconnect biblical faith principles and spiritual authority. He combined a Puritan emphasis on divine sovereignty with a willingness to engage in the new questions raised through the rise of a rational worldview. Edwards was much in demand as a spiritual director especially in the aftermath of the Great Awakening. His vivid preaching persuaded hundreds to confess their sins, repent, and desire spiritual rebirth. He has been hailed as America's first and best theologian.

Summary of Chapter 3

According to Edwards, the distinction between the gospel and theology is that the gospel is a message centered on the divine person and works of Jesus while theology is about the disciples and followers of Jesus Christ who seek to understand the gospel with their human nature and interpret it for practical life.

The important thing is how theologians were faithful to the biblical truth and continued to seek after the Lord's will to the end. Revelation 2:19 reads, "I know thy works, and love, and service, and faith, and thy patience, and thy works; and the last to be more than the first." This should be the golden rule to measure all theologians' hearts.

Edwards applied his theological synthesis in confronting two crises in the eighteenth century—the internal problem of the dying of spiritual power in the Puritan renewal movement and the problem of the church internally and institutions surrounding the church, and the emerging influence of humanistic rationalism and the secular drift of Western culture.

Edwards's great achievement was the creation of a theology which confronted both of these two crises head-on, opposing a humanist Enlightenment in society with an evangelical awakening in the church.

Edwards's arguments for a clear, Calvinistic position delayed the liberal theology which was to dominate New England in the eighteenth century. He brought together evangelistic zeal and a powerful intellectual curiosity. Quoted from Edwards's own words from *A Faithful Narrative of the Surprising Work of God* book; "There was scarcely a single person in the town, old and young, left unconcerned about the great things of the eternal world. Those who were wont to be the vainest, and loosest, and those who had been most disposed to think, and speak slightly of vital and experimental religion, were now generally subject to great awakenings. And the work of conversion was carried on in a most astonishing manner, and increased more and more; souls did, as it were, come by flocks to Jesus Christ. From day to day, for many months together, might be seen evident instances of sinners brought out of darkness into marvelous light, and delivered out of a horrible pit, and from the miry clay, and set upon a rock with a new song of praise to God in their mouths. This work of God, as it was carried on, and the number of true saints multiplied, soon made a glorious alteration in the town; so that In the spring and summer following, anno 1735, the town seemed to be full of the prance of God: it was never full of love, nor of joy, and yet so full of distress, as it was then. There were remarkable tokens of God's presence in almost every house. It was a time of joy in families on account of salvation being brought unto them; parents rejoicing over their children as new born, and husbands over their wives and wives over their husbands"

Edwards wrote "Some thoughts concerning the present Revival of religion." I quote from his memoirs.

> How common a thing has it been for a great part of a congregation to be at once moved by a mighty invisible power! And of six, eight, or ten souls to be converted to God (to all appearance) in an exercise, in whom the visible change still continues! How great an alteration has been made in some towns, yea, some populous towns, the change still abiding! And how many very vicious persons have been wrought upon, so as to become visibly new creatures! God has also made his hand very visible, and his work glorious, in the multitudes of little children that have been wrought upon. I suppose there have been some hundreds of instances of this nature of late, any one of which formerly would have looked upon so remarkable, as to be worthy to be recorded, and published through the land.
>
> The work is very glorious in its influences and effects on many who have been very ignorant and barbarous, as I before observed of the Indians and Negroes.
>
> The work is also exceeding glorious in the high attainment of Christians, in the extraordinary degrees of light, love, and spiritual joy that God has bestowed upon great multitudes. In this respect also, the land in all parts has abounded with such instances, any one of, which, if they had happened formerly, would have been thought worthy to be noticed by God's people throughout the British

dominions. The New Jerusalem in this respect has begun to come down from heaven, and perhaps never were more of the prelibation of heaven's glory given upon earth.

Edwards was well known for never having stopped being a Puritan. His efforts in revival theology were based on his genius, his religious experience, and his truthful preaching of the traditional reformed theology he inherited from Calvin. Edwards combined Calvin's "Sense of Sweetness" doctrine with his "New Sense" of regenerating and illuminating the work of the Spirit to appreciate the truth and beauty of the gospel.

Edwards was a gift of God to the awakening era, a faithful servant of the Lord who was dedicated to the theological foundations of revivals. His great and systematic works were left largely uncomplicated. In spite of all Edwards's uncomplicated theological works, he exalted the glory of God and depicted His source of absolutely perfect being with supernal beauty and love. Theologians after him appreciated Edwards's brilliant mind as a religious thinker.

The Keys to the Shaping of Edwards's Early Ministry

Solomon Stoddard (1643–1729), Edwards's maternal grandfather, was known as the "Pope of the Connecticut River Valley." He had a key role in shaping Edwards's ministry as the associate minister. Edwards recorded in his *Faithful Narrative* the five seasons of "harvests" (or revivals) that led to the growth of the Northampton church, the largest in New England outside Boston. Edwards witnessed his own spiritual harvests benefiting by serving as assistant pastor. Stoddard's personal, affectionate preaching style that aimed at moving the whole person—heart, soul, and mind—had contributed to these harvests. Edwards had learned this Puritan-style "art of prophesy" and gradually developed the excellence of rhetoric combined with verbal imagery and metaphor. To Edwards's regret, the revival lasted only a short time. His "Religious Affections" treatise recorded his insightful, pertinent discussions and reflections. He argued strongly that Christian practice in conformity to Christian rules was the principal sign of true religion.

Edwards emphasized the importance of the revival experience. He also pointed out the role of the "will, heart and affections" and that the affections motivate the heart in religious life. To him, love was the most important one among affections.

Perhaps Edwards's most famous work is his treatise "A Careful and Strict Enquiry into the Prevailing Notions of the Freedom of the Will" (1754), which was written to counter Arminian understanding of the nature of salvation.

Edwards's Followers

Edwards's writings were championed by many of his followers, including Joseph Bellamy (1719–1790), Samuel Hopkins (1701–1803), Jonathan Edwards Jr. (1745–1803), Sarah Osborn (1714–1796), John Smalley (1734–1820), and Nathaniel Emmons (1745–1840). These followers were very competent scholars and industrious workers. They were also labeled the Edwardians and were engaged in arguments with the Old Calvinists, followers of the federal or covenant theology.

Edwards and the New Divinity

> Edwards left behind a complex theological legacy; the "New Divinity" was a term of opprobrium in the 1760s, used by outsiders to stigmatize Edwards's followers as innovators. The term "Hopkinsian"-from Samuel Hopkins-took hold by the end of 1700s.

Samuel Hopkins wrote,

Edwards simply decided that he was unable to match the graceful gregariousness of those ministers who had a knack at introducing profitable, religious discourse in a free, natural, and undersigned way. Thus, he felt he would do the greatest good to souls by preaching and writing, contriving, laboring; for them above any other people under heaven. The study at Edwards's home was thronged, Hopkins said, with people seeking to lay open their spiritual concerns to him. And Edwards counseled them all. During the revival years, Edwards continued performing all of the regular duties of a minister to his flock-among them, some of these involved young people he had counseled and catechized, such as Zadok Lyman, who wed Sarah Clark on January 31, 1745.

Chapter 4

LEADERS OF THE FIRST GREAT AWAKENING

William Tennent (1673–1746)—Presbyterian, Pennsylvania

Theodore J. Frelinghuysen (1691–1748)—Dutch Reformed, New Jersey

Jonathan Edwards (1703–1758)—Congregational, Massachusetts

Gilbert Tennent (1703–1764)—Presbyterian, Pennsylvania

Shubal Stearns (1706–1771)—Baptist, southern colonies

George Whitefield (1714–1770)—Anglican, across colonial America

Samuel Davies (1723–1761)—Presbyterian, Virginia

The Theological Diversity of the Awakening Era

- The New England region: Calvinists who believed in predestination
- The New Jersey area: The Dutch Reformed starting with German Pietists
- The middle colonies: the mystical religiosity led by Rev. Gilbert, John, and William Tennent with their claim of special signs of divine favor and supernatural powers.

Edwards's and Whitefield's Impact on the Great Awakening

Both Edwards and Whitefield were critics of deism, which is theism minus miracles, or theistic naturalism. It is the idea that God got the universe going and it has run on its own steam since then. Edwards and Whitefield favored a theological and spiritual dimension to the defense of historical Christianity.

Since 1735, the amazing, divine love touched Whitefield's heart as he converted. He committed his life to the calling from God and became the great Calvinist evangelist of the eighteenth century.

Whitefield founded the English Calvinistic Methodist Connexion, whose first conference met in 1743. He centered his theology on the old English Puritan themes of original sin, justification by faith and regeneration. Sometimes he was militantly Calvinist, but he preached with rare passion for souls. **"Calvinistic Methodist"** was indeed a term with real meaning applied to him.

Following the footsteps of John Wesley's missionary vision, Whitefield answered the divine calling and came to colonial America when he was twenty-four. He visited Georgia briefly in 1738 to aid in the founding of an orphanage.

On May 24, 1738, John Wesley experienced personal conversion and started to develop a theology based on the Moravians' emphasis on salvation by faith. (Wesley also had his law's belief in moral perfectionism before he encountered the Moravians.)

When Whitefield returned from his second trip to the colonies in 1739, his reputation as a dramatic preacher preceded him. The colonies' newspapers that had detailed almost all his everyday events had built anticipation for his tour of the colonies. Whitefield always made sure that his sermons and journals were widely available to the newspapers.

Whitefield made his first visit to Philadelphia in November

THE GREAT AWAKENING

1739 (for his second of his seven trips to the colonies). His original purpose was to collect donations for supplies for his orphanage in Georgia. During his nine-day stay in Philadelphia, he put the city's residents in a frenzy. Whitefield visited Benjamin Franklin in Philadelphia in 1739 and recorded the occasion in his autobiography. Whitefield was the first permitted to preach in some of their churches. However, the churches' clergy disliked him and soon refused to provide him their pulpits, so he had to preach in the fields.

> The multitudes of all sects and denominations that attended his sermons were enormous, and it was matter of speculation to me, who was one of the number, to observe the extraordinary influence of his oratory on his hearts, and how much they admired and respected him, notwithstanding his common abuse of them, by assuring them they were naturally *half beasts* and *half devils*.
>
> Franklin said of the Great Awakening in general: Never did the people show so great a willingness to attend sermons. Religion is become the subject of most conversation." "It was wonderful to see the change soon made in the manners of our inhabitants. From being thoughtless or indifferent about religion, it seemed as if the entire world were growing religious, so that one could not walk through the town in the evening without hearing psalms in different families of every street.

Whitefield had a loud and clear voice, benefiting from his early youth's training on the theater stage. He articulated words and sentences perfectly, and he was heard and understood at a great distance.

On September 14, 1740, the Boston newspapers carried advertisements of numerous books and tracts about Whitefield; during the next seventy-three days, he traveled eight hundred miles and preached 130 sermons. Whitefield was greeted everywhere by great throngs. His touring extended all over New England; newspapers reports from that time portray Whitefield preaching to crowds of 8,000 people every day for month-long stretches.

Edwards wrote to Whitefield on February 1740 and offered his pulpit to him; Edwards hoped Whitefield's preaching would spark another revival like the previous one of 1734–35.

Edwards's Observation of Whitefield

> But in a series of sermons Edwards preached during and after Whitefield's visit, we find that Jonathan's awe of the Grand Itinerant was more reserved than Sarah's. Edwards worried that Whitefield's stirring; flamboyant preaching style was particularly apt to produce religious hypocrites. Such preaching raised the affections (the heartfelt convictions) of hearers by its force of argument, "aptness of expression," and "the fervency, and liveliness, and beautiful gesture of the preacher." But would such last?"

> On Sunday August 24, 1746, Whitefield delivered a sermon in Philadelphia:

> Sermon of "The Seed of the Woman, and the Seed of Serpent."

> [Remarks written by Ola Elizabeth Winslow]

> Scripture Reference from Genesis 3:15: "And I will put Enmity between thee and Woman, and between thee Seed and Her Seed, it shalt bruise thy Head and

thou shalt bruise His Heel."

Typical Whitefield sermons always left his audience exhausted.

Some were struck pale as death," goes one report, "others wringing their hands; others lie on the ground, others sinking into the arms of their friends, and most lifting up their eyes toward heaven, and crying out to God." Whitefield gave "church-going America ... its first taste of theater under the flag of salvations," "Ola Elizabeth Winslow has remarked, taking care to add, however, that theatrics alone did not explain Whitefield's success: he arrived in America long after the seeds of the Great awakening had been planted and merely put in his suckle and claim the harvest.

Franklin published *The General Magazine and Historical Chronicle for All the British Plantation* in America on January 1741 in Philadelphia. He merged it with a new magazine named *The General Magazine* in February 1741. It was a curious anthology of American literary primitives for 1741. The three chief topics dealt with were England and the British War, the problem of paper currency, and the Great Awakening as recently proclaimed by George Whitefield.

Franklin, himself no public speaker, carefully noted Whitefield's oratory. "He had a loud and clear voice, and articulated his words and sentences so perfectly that he might be heard and understood at a great distance, especially as his auditoriums, however numerous, observed the most exact silence. He preached one evening from the top of the courthouse steps, which are in the middle of Market Street and on the west side of Second Street, which crosses it at right angles. Being among the hindmost in Market Street, I had the curiosity to learn how far he could be heard, by

Retiring backwards down the street towards the river I found his voice distinct until I came near Front Street, when some noise in that street obscured it. Imagining then a semicircle, of which my distance should be the radius, and that it were filled with auditors to each of whom I allowed two square feet, I computed that he might be heard by more than thirty thousand. This reconciled me to the newspaper accounts of his having preached to twenty-five thousand people in the fields, and to the ancient stories of generals haranguing whole armies, of which I had sometimes doubted.

New Milestones in Whitefield's Pulpit Preaching

Preaching before Whitefield arrived was defined in medieval or classical categories. Benjamin Franklin also recorded another event of Whitefield's: "It was wonderful to see the change soon made in the manner of our inhabitants." Franklin was moved enough by one of Whitefield's sermons to empty his pockets when the collection plate was passed.

According to Franklin's estimate, over 30,000 showed up to one of the great meetings.

> From being thoughtless and indifferent about religion, it seemed as if the entire world was growing religious, so that one could not walk through Philadelphia in the evening without hearing Psalms sung in different families on every street.

The young English Anglican itinerant preacher's tours were huge events at that time. So many people showed up as if by magic to hear him preach the good news of the new birth. Whenever he preached, crowds of unprecedented size and inclusivity appeared. Whitefield had the gift of an unusual sensitivity to what it took to draw audiences. His heart-to-heart style of delivery touched countless souls for the Lord. Over the course of his career, Whitefield preached to audiences that must have numbered in the millions. Often, he would spend up to forty hours a week in the pulpit.

Analysis of Whitefield's Sermon on Repentance

Whitfield's sermon on repentance drew its title from "Except ye repent, ye shall all likewise perish" (Luke 13:3). Its opening statement was this.

> When we consider how heinous and aggravating our offense are in the sight of God, that they bring down his wrath upon our heads, and occasion us to live under his indignation; how ought we thereby to be deterred from evil, or at least engaged to study to repent thereof and not commit the same again! But man is so thoughtless of an eternal state, and has so little consideration of the welfare of his immortal soul, that he can sin without any thought that he must give an account of his actions at the Day of Judgment. If he, at times, has any reflections on his behavior, they do not drive him to true repent.
>
> He may, for a short time, refrain from falling into some gross sins which he had lately committed; but then, when the temptation comes again with power, he is carried away with the lust; and thus he goes on promising and resolving, and in breaking both his

resolutions and his promises, as fast almost as he has made them.

This is highly offensive to God; it is mocking of him. My brethren, when grace is given us to repent truly, we shall turn wholly unto God; and let me beseech you to repent of your sins, for the time is hastening when you will have neither time nor call to repent; there is none in the grave, wither we are going. But do not be afraid, for God often receives the greatest sinner to mercy through the merits of Christ Jesus. This magnifies the riches of his free grace; and should be an encouragement for you, who are great and notorious sinners, to repent, for he will have mercy upon you, if you through Christ return unto him.

Apostle Paul was an eminent instance of this. He speaks of himself as "the chief of sinners," and he declares hoe God showed mercy unto him. Christ loves to show mercy unto sinners, and if you repent, he will have mercy upon you. But as no word is more mistaken than that of repentance, I shall: Show you what the nature of repentance is. Consider the several parts and causes of repentance. I shall give you some reasons, why repentance is necessary to salvation. And Exhort all of you, high and low, rich and poor, one with another, to endeavor after repentance.

Whitefield emphasized the importance of true repentance without compromising the biblical truth of the Lord: "Except ye repent, ye shall all likewise perish" (Luke 13:3). Jesus addressed His words to the disciples in the hearing of the multitude. He warned them against hypocrisy, the characteristic spirit of the Pharisees (verses

1–3). Jesus also encouraged them with the assurance of God's loving care in this world (verses 4–7).

Whitefield went directly to his point, "Repent or Perish." There is no middle ground. This is the absolute truth of the gospel. Whitefield started his address with a friendly tone by including his listeners with the words "When we consider …" Togetherness is a key feeling of connectedness to break the ice between him and the listeners. Whitefield applied Jesus' truth by saying,

> First, you who never have truly repented of your sins, and never have truly forsaken your lust, be not offended if I speak plainly to you: for it is love, love to your souls that constrain me to speak. I shall lay before you your danger, and the misery to which you are exposed, while you remain impenitent in sin. And oh that this may be a means of making you fly to Christ for pardon and forgiveness.

Whitefield expressed the compassionate approach as in the

> Apostle Paul at *Rome* book; "Therefore, while you are going on in a course of sins and unrighteousness, *I beseech* you, my brethren, to think of the consequence that will attend your thus misspending your precious time. Your souls are worth being concerned about, for if you can enjoy all the pleasures and diversions of life, at death you must leave them; that will put you an end to all your worldly concerns. And will it not be deplorable to have your good things here, all your earthly, sensual, devilish pleasures, which you have been so much taken up with, all over, gnaw at your very soul.

Whitefield summarized at his sermon with,

A. The great love of Christ.

Let the love of Jesus to you, keep you also humble; do not be high minded, keep close unto the Lord, observe the rules which the Lord Jesus Christ has given in his word, and let not the instructions be lost which you are capable of giving. Oh consider what reason you have to be thankful to the Lord Jesus Christ for giving you that repentance you yourselves had need of; a repentance which workth by love. Now you find more pleasure in walking with God one hour, than in all your former carnal delights, and all the pleasure of sin. Oh the joy you feel in your own souls, which all the men of this world and all the devils in hell, though they were to combine together, could not destroy. Then fear not their wrath or malice, for through many tribulations we must enter into glory.

B. An invitation to Christ's grace of repentance with a warning and exhortation

Oh, what shall I say to you, to make you come to Jesus? I have showed you the dreadful consequences of not repenting of your sins; and if, after all I have said, you are resolved to persist, your blood will be requested at your own hands; but I hope better things of you, and things that accompany salvation. Let me beg you to pray in good earnest for the grace of repentance. I may never see your faces again; but at the Day of Judgment I will meet you. There you will either bless God that ever you were moved to repentance; or else this sermon, though in a field, will be as a swift witness against you. Repent, repent, therefore, my dear brethren, as John the Baptist, and your blessed Redeemer himself earnest exhorted, and turn from your evil ways, and the Lord will have mercy on you.

C. The closing prayer

Show them, oh Father, wherein they have offended thee; make them to see their own vileness, and that they are lost and undone without true repentance. Oh give them that repentance, we beseech thee, that they may turn from sin unto thee, the living and true God. These things, and whatever else thou seest needful for us, we entrust that thou would bestow upon us, on account of what dear Jesus Christ has done and suffered; to whom, with thyself and the Holy Spirit, three persons and one God, be ascribed, as is most due, all power, glory, might, majesty, and dominion, now, henceforth, and forevermore. Amen.

I was deeply moved by the sincerity and humility of Whitefield's closing prayer; he gave God the honor and authority to show how he respected and was thankful for the magnificent salvation plan we received in Christ's redemption paid at the cross. It is finished; praise the heavenly Father.

Whitefield was a master at using the media; other than his masterful eloquence when it came to innovating listeners, Whitefield also proved to be a master of the art of self-promotion through the mass media. He spent time with reporters almost everywhere he preached.

Before the awakening era, newspapers did not typically include religion in their subject matter other than religiously related essays on moral issues, for instance. But almost from the beginning of his preaching career, Whitefield enlisted many friendly and unfriendly editors in many of his campaigns to publicize his tours of proclaiming the gospel. He worked with advance men who would send notices to newspapers describing his past campaigns' highlights and his coming to their regions.

To traditional churchmen, the secular newspapers represented an alien presence that was at best indifferent to and at worst a threat to traditional religious print. But to Whitefield, it represented a novel form of public outreach that could reach customers and consumers who eluded the nets of printed sermons and settled churches. Again, we see a commercialization and commoditization of preaching and ministry. In utilizing the secular newspapers and magazines, Whitefield was presenting religion as a popular commodity that could not compete so much with the goods and services of this world.

Perhaps one of Whitefield's great contributions to the awakening era was his innovative approach to preaching. He knew exactly how to effectively use plain language to connect with large crowds.

The highlight of Whitefield's ministry was at the famous Cambuslang Awakening in 1742, when a record 20,000 and 30,000 people gathered to hear him preach. This was followed by mass weeping and repentance for one and half hours.

Immense Benefits

Whitefield made subsequent visits (1744–1748, 1751–1752, 1754–1755, 1763–1765, and 1769–1770) and followed the same extraordinary pattern until he died in Newburyport, Massachusetts, in 1770.

In total, Whitefield spent nine years in America and a full two years sailing the Atlantic. He woke up daily at 4:00 a.m. for devotions and often preached twice a day and three times on

Sundays. He was a very sincere, dedicated, single-minded man who was always thinking about his Master's business. God's grace and blessing gave such a great evangelist as Whitefield the gift to impact America.

Whitefield's Marvelous Preaching Ministry

It was estimated that Whitefield's ministry covered almost every town in England, Scotland, and Wales. He crossed the Atlantic seven times and won countless souls in Boston, New York, and Philadelphia. According to Christian historians' estimation, Whitefield's 18,000 power-packed messages set enormous records nobody in religious history could even come close to. He was able to draw audiences from all denominations due to his powerful presence and ministry.

Whitefield and other itinerant preachers who followed in his wake preached wherever and whenever God opened for them opportunities to proclaim the gospel. Whitefield became America's great gift to Protestantism.

By the end of 1740, Whitefield had toured across the southern and middle colonies as well as New England. Thousands of admirers showed up wherever he preached, and invariably, "The groans and outcries of the wounded were such that my voice could not be heard." Whitefield left for England at the beginning of 1741, but the awakening movement continued at fever pitch across the land. The seeds of devout evangelical fervor were planted in the south during the awakenings. The Baptists in particular had a remarkable impact on the south ever since the Great Awakening. \

> Anglicans and Quakers and to some degree the Baptists-"those poor, bigoted, ignorant, prejudiced people"- as the evangelist Eleazar Wheelock called them, watched the frenzy from a distance, but few

others remained calm. Even the pietist sects among the German-speaking people, though they held aloof from the Whitefield revival, did not escape altogether; their Awakening was initiated by Count Nicolaus Zinzendorf, who sought (and failed) to unite the host of German sects into a single association.

The Baptists, who believed in democracy and emotional religion, probably gained more members than did any other denomination chiefly from the Congregationalists in New England and Anglicans.

It is believed that the Great Awakening ended by 1744, but Whitefield continued to attract huge audiences wherever he went during his following five trips to America. However, between 1740 and 1741, the awakening movement had had a great affect that transcended all social, geographic, urban, and rural boundaries; the impact was tremendous, and the religious life of Americans would never again the same.

Dr. Peter Hammond of the Reformation Society mentioned Whitefield in his article [4]:

> Whitefield has been attributed with pioneering non-denominational, international, para-church ministry. He preached to the heart, and demanded a response. He utilized the media and blazed the trail which future generations of Evangelical Revivalists, chaplains, youth and student para-church leaders and Christian charities have followed. By all accounts, those who were awakened by his burning words to a sense of their spiritual needs and who came to Christ as a result of his Biblical preaching number in, at least, the hundreds of thousands. The lives changed by the Great Evangelical Awakening

[4] Reformation Society (South Africa) magazine, 1960

launched through his itinerant preaching ministry are incalculable.

Some Quotable saying of Whitefield

God forbid that I should travel with anybody a quarter of an hour without speaking of Christ to them.

> I hope to grow rich in heaven by taking care of orphans on earth.

> Young Christians are like little rivulets that make a large noise and have shallow water; old Christians are like deep water that makes little noise, carries a good load and gives not away.

> Suffering times are a Christian's best improving times.

> In mighty signs and wonders, by the power of the Spirit of God ... I have fully preached the Gospel of Christ, and so I have made it my aim to preach the gospel, not where Christ was named, lest I should build on another man's foundation. (Romans 15:19–20)

Edwards's Preaching Style For decades, Edwards was well known as "a man on fire for God." The years between 1740 and 1742 were the height of awakening; the fire of God was falling everywhere in New England.

Edwards's delivery was recorded by Stephen William.

> We went to Enfield where we met dear Mr. Edwards of Northampton who preached a most awakening sermon from Deuteronomy 32:35, and before the sermon was done there was a great moaning and crying that went out through the whole House ...

"What shall I do to be saved," "Oh, I am going to Hell," "Oh what shall I do for Christ," and so forth. So yet ye minister was obliged to desist, ye shrieks and cry were piercing and amazing."

Edwards was a great reformer in moral issues as well as the revival of religion; his famous sermons included "Sinner in the Hands of an Angry God," "The Torments of the Wicked in Hell," "No Occasion of Grief to the Saints in Heaven," and "The Final Judgment." He frightened his audiences to death. His passive style of delivery seemed cold but ultimately carried a message of hope and salvation.

Edwards was evoking greater seriousness and solemnity in people and prompting people to make religion a far more important aspect of their lives.

In October 16, 1740, Whitefield went to Northampton to see Edwards and converse with him regarding the work of God in. He stayed with Edwards until October 20.

Recollections According to Edwards

Edwards's most pressing responsibility was preaching to his congregation. He invested heavily in the preparation of sermons, which often gave the first public expression to ideas developed in his notebooks. During his lifetime Edwards published eighteen sermons. The most famous of all was his Enfield sermon that continues to attract widespread attention today. Of greater significance, perhaps, is the "Farewell Sermon" in which he revealed his personal perspective upon the Northampton controversy. Two of Edwards's sermon series, A History of the Work of Redemption and Charity and Its Fruits that were published as treatises after his death. Today there is extent a collection of approximately thirteen hundred manuscript sermons.

Very few preachers could provoke sharper reactions than Edwards did; for him, biblical exposition was the soul, marrow, and sinew of his purposeful proclaiming the gospel.

John Newton (1725–1807) was asked once, who was the greatest divine of his era? He replied unhesitatingly, "Edwards."

Analysis of Edwards's Sermon "Sinners in the Hands of an Angry God"

"Their foot shall slide in due time" (Deuteronomy 32:35). In this verse, God threatens the wicked, unbelieving Israelites, God's chosen people. Edwards said, "The expression I have chosen for my text, *their foot shall slide in due time*,

seems to imply the following things, relating to the punishment and destruction to which these wicked Israelites were exposed." Edwards explained in his text,

1. That they were always exposed to destruction. and 2. It implies that they were always exposed to sudden unexpected destruction. As he that walks in slippery places is every moment liable to fall, he cannot foresee one moment whether he shall stand or fall the next; and when he does fall, he falls at once without warning: which is also expressed in Psalm 73:18, 19: "Surely thou set them in slippery

places, thou casted them down into destructions. How are they brought into desolation as a moment?

3. Another thing implied is, that they are liable to fall of themselves, without being thrown down by the hands of another; as he that stands or walks on slippery ground needs nothing but his own weight to throw him down. 4. That the reason why they are not fallen already, and do not fall now, is only that God's appointed time is not come.

The observation from the words that I would now insist upon is this-"There is nothing that keeps wicked men at any one moment out of hell, but the mere pleasure, his arbitrary will, restrained by no obligation, hindered by no manners of difficult, any more than if nothing else but God's mere will had in the least degree, or in any respect whatsoever, any hand in the preservation of wicked men one moment.

Main Paragraph

O Sinner! Consider the fearful danger you are in: it is a great furnace of wrath, a wide and bottomless pit, full of the fire of wrath, that you are held over in the hand of that God, whose wrath is provoked and incensed as much against you, against many of the damned in hell. You hang by a slender thread, with the flames of divine wrath flashing about it, and ready every moment to singe it, and burn it asunder; and you have no interest in any Mediator, and nothing to lay hold of to save yourself, nothing that you ever have done, nothing you can do, to induce God to spare you one moment.

The bow of God's wrath is bent, and the arrow made ready on the strings, and justice bends the arrow at your heart, and strains the bow, and it is nothing but the mere pleasure of God, and that of an angry God, without any promise or obligation at all, that keeps the arrow one moment from being made drunk with your blood. Thus all you that have never passed under a great change of heart, by the mighty power of the Spirit of God upon your souls; all you that were never born again, and made new creatures, and raised from being dead in sin, to a state of new, and before altogether unexpected light and life, are in the hands of angry God.

Edwards then wrote,

> The observation from the words that I would now insist upon is-"There is nothing that keeps wicked men at any one moment out of hell, but the mere pleasure of God." I mean his *sovereign* pleasure, his arbitrary will, restrained by no obligation, hindered by no manner of difficulty, and more than if nothing else but God's mere will had in the least degree, or in any respect whatsoever, any band in the preservation of vicious men one moment.

Edwards's preaching power resided in his selected words delivered in his clear and calm modulation from all his completed written texts.

> Edwards compared sinners to a spider, a "loathsome insect" suspended over an eternal fire, a "bottomless pit, full of the fire of wrath," held only by a slender

thread that at any moment might give way. As for "angry God," Edwards meant that-"God's wrath required no further provocation, nor was there any necessity for divine action. On the contrary, unrepentant sinners would not be thrown into hell but would be allowed simply to fall of their own weight to those depths, where they would endure torture that would not, and could never, be relieved, in Edwards's frighteningly powerful portrayal of the meaning of the infinite. Only the hand of God held sinners up from the pit of eternal misery. When God withheld support, they fell. They were condemned already.

Harriet Beecher Stowe complained that Edwards's sermon on sin and suffering was "refined poetry of torture." In fact, Edwards said it very clear: according to the Bible, God was moved by love and wrath. However, Edwards did not write another sermon like "Sinners." More typical of Edwards's preaching focused on "A Divine and Supernatural Light." The characteristic of his sermons, which had the Puritan style of a very careful exposition of points and subpoints, made it easy for recording people to write them down.

In the meantime, Patrick Sherry, the historian, argued that Edwards made beauty more central to theology than others in the history of Christian thought.

The "New Lights" and the "Old Lights"

Wherever there is fire there is also smoke. Many excess accompanied the revival as people experienced highly unusual spiritual phenomenon. Sometimes, during sermons, they screamed and dropped unconscious to the floor. Edwards's own wife sat trance-like in a corner of their living room for long periods, unable to move, utterly overwhelmed by God's love. Reverend Wheelock's diary for October 1741 is typical. "The zeal of some too furious: they tell of many visions, revelations, and many strong impressions upon the imagination ... Preached twice with enlargement, Many cried out; many stood trembling; the whole assembly very solemn.

Many scholars considered Edwards America's greatest philosopher before the twentieth century.

> Edwards was arguably this continent's greatest theologian ever. One member of his greatness is Yale University Press' critical edition of his works, which has twenty-six volumes—but even that represents only half of his written products. Another token of Edwards's importance is the three-volume *Encyclopedia of the American Religious Experience*, which contains far more references to Edwards than any other single figure.

Divisions among the Churches

The Great Awakening caused divisions among the churches; some were immediate and direct results while many others were long-term and indirect results.

> In the aftermath of the Great Awakening of 1740-41, Old Light opposition to evangelical revivals solidified, as did a self-conscious Arminian perspective among many in the same Old Light party. The revivals had thus the unintended effect of bringing permanent polarization between evangelical and liberal clergy.

Both sides, then, and many scholars since, have wrongly assumed that Edwards's affections were the same thing as "emotions." But emotions for Edwards were only one dimension of human experience shaped by affections, along with thinking and choosing. Edwards argued that true religious affections sometimes choose against emotional feeling, such as when Jesus chose not to yield to his feelings of fear in the garden of Gethsemane. When "passion" overwhelms one's better judgment, as in a fit of rage, emotions are in fact opposed to true religious affections. Furthermore, Edwards linked affections to objects, while emotions may or may not have an object. In current English usage, the statement "I am emotional" need not imply an object of emotion. But the assertion "I am affectionate" raised the question, "Towards what or whom?"

Edwards's Evaluation of the Awakening

Edwards took the lead early in careful defense of the awakening at Yale in his 1741 commencement sermon, *The Distinguishing Marks of a Work of the Spirit of God*. Not denying flaws, Edwards provided criteria for his belief that the revival was a genuine work of God. As the excesses of the revival multiplied and the attacks grew sharper, Edwards enlarged his defense into a major work, "Some Thoughts Concerning the Present Revival of Religion in the New England" (1742). He admitted that the revival had some features that were not of God and that ought to be purged.

With great thoroughness, he then marshaled evidence that the revival was genuine. He claimed that it had brought an increase in concern for eternal things, improved moral behavior, awakened consciences, cultivated soberness among youth, increased strictness in Sabbath observance, focused closer attention to the Bible, won many converts, helped in the gathering of the Native Americans, and speeded the advancement of Christ's kingdom. In the light of all the evidence, he asked, who could doubt that for the most part the revival was really the work of God?

> Whitefield for his part had also contributed to controversy over the revival when he confided in one issue of his published *Journal* that "a great number of ministers" in New England was spiritually unfit. When such statements found their way into print in April 1741, there was cascade of anti-Whitefield pamphlets and letters to the editor.

Whitefield's Controversy in Carolina

Commissary Alexander Garden (1685–1756) of the Anglican Church in Carolina witnessed some congregational growth during his tenure, but the spiritual condition of the church in general was greatly dimmed by unchecked competition.

> *Whitefield* attended one service in Garden's church (after the 1740), then advised the people to worship in the dissenting meeting house "since the Gospel was not preached in the Church." The revivalist added that perhaps the society should send no more missionaries to the Carolina since those that had been sent were such poor representatives: "the established Church is in excellent order as to externals," Whitefield wrote in 1740, but its chief ministers were in fact "bigots." Commissary Garden succeeded in summoning an ecclesiastical court in Charlestown and tried to suspend Whitefield from exercising the ministerial office

of an Anglican minister. Garden informed the Bishop of London that, if it were in his power, he would excommunicate Whitefield altogether. For his evangelizer only weaken the church further, holding it up to ridicule, encouraging illiterate and untrained men to imitate him in a traveling ministry, and creating the illustration that salvation was "a sudden, instantaneous Work" rather than "a gradual and cooperative work of the Holy Spirit, joining in our understandings and leading us on by Reason and Persuasion." But it was not in Garden's power either to excommunicate Whitefield or to prevent his continuing ministry. He did succeed in driving Whitefield even more fully into the arms of the dissenters, Charlestown's Baptists, Presbyterians, and Congregationalists welcome him warmly.

The most immediate consequence of the awakening was the splitting of the Congregationalists into Old Lights, those who hold the older views, and the New Lights, who favored Edwards's theory.

At the early awakening years, as the debates aroused between New Lights and the Old Lights, they offered different evidence in support of their positions. The Old Lights considered the New Lights' itinerant evangelism, extemporaneous preaching, and lay exhorting as dangerous innovations that created confusion and many errors. The Old lights believed the New Lights damaged believers' minds and presented only part of God's truth.

> Yet if Edwards was warning conservative pastors not to reject the revival outright, he was also cautioning radical New Light preachers, some of whom reveled in the bodily manifestations and exalted spiritual experiences they had witnessed. His argument cut

both ways. In effect, he was urging Old Lights not to reject a revival as spurious if it involved bodily and visionary experiences, and New Lights not to embrace a revival as genuine merely because it exhibited these phenomena ... Edwards's appeal for moderation in *Distinguishing Marks* had only limited success. Pro-revival students at Yale College flouted college authorities in November 1741.

Rector Clap made an example of one of Edwards's admirers, David Brainerd into a martyr, by removing him from Yale. This act of expulsion only served to turn Brainerd into a martyr, and the uproar grew so great that Clap had to suspend classes in Aril 1742. Pro-revival forces in Connecticut responded by opening a short-lived rival college in New London, called the "Shepherd's Tent." Allen Guelzo comments: "It is easy to sympathize with Whitefield and Tennent as the underdog. But Whitefield and Tennent's decision to turn itinerant and preach without permission from the local ministry subverted what little order ministries and magistrates could hope to impose on the wild rim of British Empire." The New Light proponents were challenging ministerial authority and the standing order of churches by offering parishioners their own choice of which preachers to hear and churches to attend.

The Great Debate: Edwards versus Chauncy

Between 1741 and 1743 their so-called debate was not really a debate at all;

Edwards never directly addressed his adversary, and

much of his argument was devoted to repudiating not the positions of his Bostonian opponent but the even more problematic arguments of Edwards's supposed allies among the radical New Lights. But Chauncy did address Edwards's arguments directly, especially in his *Reasonable Thoughts on the State of Religion in New England* (1743), which ran to more than 400 pages. Not only the title of that work but also its organization and topics were meant to counter Edwards's Some *Thoughts Concerning the Present Revival*, which had appeared the previous ... some of Chauncy's sermons contained an evangelical strain almost as strong as that found in Edwards's famous Sinners in the *Hands of an Angry God*. In June of 1742, Chauncy's Sermon on The New Creature Described contained the following call to conversion: *Who hath bewitched you?* O Sinners, that you are thus lost to all sense of your own safety and interest! Be convinced of your danger. You are certainly in a state of dreadful and amazing hazard. You are the persons marked out, as it were, by name, in the revelations of God, for an exclusion from the kingdom of heaven: And if you live and die in your present condition, you will surely be made miserable without mercy and remedy. It is no tale I am now telling you; No, *but the very truth of the true and faithful God*. O realize it to be so! And awake out of your security. Awake thou that sleepest, and call on thy God!"

Opponents' Views

The major voice against the Edwards and revivalists came from Rev. Charles Chauncy (1705–1787). He was best known for his writings that challenged the genuineness of the violent conversations accompanying the Great Awakening. Chauncy held liberal views on both regarding the religion and the politics and attacked the revival views. Chauncy himself was actually moved from Arminism to Universalism; he followed their doctrine, which proclaimed the "salvation of all men to be 'the grand thing aimed at in the scheme of God.'" In Chauncy's view, the doctrine of eternal damnation no longer made sense.

> The Old Lights leader Charles Chauncy opposed the exhorters for "spiriting people to Schism and faction," but a counter-convention of ministers friendly to the Awakening had already cautioned their adherents not to indulge "a Spirit of Censoriousness, Uncharitableness, and rush rash judging the state of others." Opponents of the movement decried George Whitefield for his violations of the cannons of peace and emotional control, but many of Whitefield's most prominent ministerial supports also denounced emotional extravagance and Whitefield himself issued a similar disavowal.

Chauncy rebuked Whitefield's censoriousness and lampooned and mercilessly attacked Edwards's revivalism; he emerged as the spokesman for the critics of the awakening.

Interesting enough, many Old Lights were simultaneously liberal and conservative. Theologically, the Old Lights were much more liberal than were their revivalism counterparts. In fact, Charles Chauncy, the most outspoken and vitriolic of all Edwards's critics, later founded the Unitarian Church, but his cultural conservatism came through in his nickname, Old Brick. Chauncy denounced the qualification of the New Light preachers as those "most commonly raw, illiterate, weak and conceited young men or lads."

Chauncy's opposition was respectable and sufficient; he was

strongly against any display of emotion in religion. He believed that religion was a sensible thing and that the last thing it should produce was emotional disturbance. There was a strong reaction to the emotional revivalism of preachers such as Whitefield and Edwards.

Edwards accepted Chauncy's challenge with writings reminding him that religion involved the whole man, emotions and reason included. Edwards argued that they must expect the Spirit of God to work through channel such as revivals.

Edwards also questioned what Chauncy meant by reason and a good moral life. Edwards thought Chauncy held a very shallow view of reason and morality. His defense of the revivals and of emotion in religion rested on a broad argument that included God and the nature of reality.

Chauncy never answered Edwards. Consequently, the revivalists stayed behind the defense of Edwards and went on in their way. However, the New Lights stressed the results of their efforts—the turnout of the crowds, the numbers of conversions, and the increase in charitable giving provided compelling evidence of the genuine nature of revivalism.

Favorable Views

In 1741, the height of the awakening era, Rev. William Cooper, a well-known preacher from Boston, said, "The golden showers have been restrained, few sons have been born to God, and the hearts of Christians not so quickened, warned and refreshed under the ordinances, as they have been." But then, Copper continued,

> The Lord whom we have sought has suddenly come to his temple. The dispensation of grace we are now under is certainly such as neither we nor our father have seen, and in some circumstances so wonderful,

that I believe there has not been the like since the extraordinary pouring of the Spirit immediately after our Lord's ascension ... the apostolically times seem to have returned upon us.

Isaac Backus (1724–1806) was "a Baptist minister who was being converted during the revival, pastured a Separate Congregational Church for many years, spoke of 'our Edwards's in approving Edwards's Calvinistic defense of the revival."

Edwards and Richard Baxter believed that theology found its true expression in pastoral care and the nurture of believers' souls.

Edwards's "A Treatise Concerning Religious Affections"

This treatise was one of Edwards's major writings in defending the revivals against the Old Lights' attacks during the peak of the awakening. After this writing, Edwards became a well-known evangelist of his time. He argued,

> Essential to Christianity were proper religious affections. Either our love and desires were directed toward God as revealed in Christ, or they were directed elsewhere. For one's heart to change, one's affections must be changed. Only God could change the heart. What the preacher could do, however, was to help provide the occasion for sinners to get a glimpse at what God was like.

Rivalry among Denominations during the Great Awakening

Other than Congregationalists and Baptists, who were split into two camps, the revivalists also split the middle-colony Presbyterians.

Proponents of revivals walked out of the Synod of

Philadelphia and formed a rival Synod of New York in 1745. The revivalists demanded higher standard for ministers in personal life and guarantees that their ministers were indeed "born again." Only moral and regenerate ministers preach with conviction, they argued. The breach between the two synods was not healed until 1758.

Edwards combined the Puritan emphasis on the divine sovereignty with a willingness to engage with the new questions being raised through the rise of a rational worldview. His theology found its practical expression particularly in his ethics.

Edwards's sermon series on 1 Corinthians 13 was published in 1746 as "Charity and Its Fruits."

> Their consciousness was stricken with their unworthiness. Edwards did not leave a single loophole. God's way with man was grounded in the very nature of things, for he was the creator and sustainer of all things. Reason and conscience both pointed to the justice of his treatment of men.

The Foundations of Edwards's Theology

> But Jonathan Edwards, who first preached the revival in Northampton, Mass., in 1733, was also in the mainstream of the Erasmian intellectual tradition. He was the pupil, at New Haven, of Samuel Johnson, whose work reflected the liberation from the ancient theological system as it was still taught in the seventeenth century-"a curious cobweb of distinctions and definitions", as he termed it. Johnson traced his own intellectual birth to the reading of Bacon's *Advancement of*

Learning, which he says left him "like one at once emerging out of a glimmer of twilight into the full sunshine of open day". "He (Edwards) read and admired Bishop Berkeley's attempt to reconcile idealism, reason and Christian belief, and he defended "natural" law, holding morality to be "the same thing as the religion of Nature", not indeed discoverable without revelation but "founded on the first principles of reason and nature". Edwards read Locke's Essay *Concerning Human Understanding* with more pleasure "than the most greedy miser finds when gathering up handfuls of silver and gold from some newly-discovered treasure". But he brought to Locke's methods of reasoning the warmth and the emotionalism they lacked. This might be termed providential: Locke was writing after a successful revolution, Edwards before one, at a time when unifying and energizing emotions were necessary to create a popular will for change. Much of his writing is capable of a political, as well as a theological interpretation.

Edwards combined basically Calvinist theological heritage with Neoplatonic influences; he combined this with his utilization of the philosophical systems of Locke and Berkeley; this made him a unique thinker.

Three Major Areas of Edwards's Theology

Calvinism: The Doctrines and Teaching of John Calvin or His Followers

Edwards, the prince of Puritans, wrote over six hundred sermons (they still exist in manuscript form). Among his most well-known and influential works are "On the Nature of True Virtue," "On Freedom of the Will," "The Great Christian Doctrine of Original Sin Defended," and "A Treatise Concerning Religious Affections."

Edwards's View of Calvinism

There is no question that Edwards was a Calvinist theologian; interestingly enough, he also claimed the heritage of his New England forebears. He requested that his followers not refer to him as a Calvinist if they meant he was dependent on his own thoughts. As we read Edwards's writings, there is evidence that his Puritan tradition drew as much from the Rhineland reformers as it did from Calvin.

Edwards's Seriousness of God's Wrath

In "The Jonathan's Works, Volume 2," one of many fine chapters in *The End of the Wicked Contemplated by the Righteous*, Edwards quoted Revelation 18:20.

> Rejoice over her, thou heaven, and ye holy apostles and prophets; for God hath avenged you and her." Edwards pointed out, "In this chapter we have a very particular account of the fall of Babylon, or the antichristian church, and of the vengeance of God execute upon her. It is not only the sight of God's wrath executed on those wicked men who are of antichristian church, which will be occasion of rejoicing to the saints in glory, but also the sight of the destruction of all God's whether they have been the followers of antichrist or not, that alters not the case, if they have been the enemies of God, and of Jesus Christ. All wicked men will at last be destroyed together, as being united in the same

cause and interest, as being all of Satan's army. They will all stand together at the day judgment, as being all of the same company.

Two of Edwards's works, "The End for which God created the World" and "The Nature of True Virtue," reflected his deeply Neoplatonic thought. He wrote, "Religious man gives himself to transcendent beauty." Hence, it seems to me the core value of Christianity is to lead believers to the transcendent beauty.

Edwards's main theme of theology revolved around God's glory: "There is no question whatever that is of greater important to mankind." Edwards wrote, "What is the nature of true religion?" He answered that question in "A Treatise Concerning Religious Affections," the most subtle and sophisticated defense of the awakening and the role of emotion in religious life. In it, he argued,

> Deep emotion was not just legitimate in a religion, it was essential to genuine religion. For without the emotions or "affections," one is not moved, one's life is not altered. Religion was not a matter of intellectual apprehension alone, not a matter of doctrinal knowledge alone, not a matter of mere propositions. Faith rested upon knowledge, but moved beyond the faculty of understanding to the faculty of the will or what we often speak of as the heart, Edwards explained that to have a change of mind was not the same as to a change of heart. The latter involved deep feeling, new direction, and transformed life.

Edwards acknowledged the "sense of the heart."

Spiritual wisdom and grace is the highest and most excellent gift that ever God Bestows on any creature," He pointed out clearly that-"It is not a thing that belongs to reason; it is not a speculative thing, but depends on the sense of the heart.

Deists claimed that human action originated from either good or bad thinking. Edwards, however, insisted that the source of human motivation lay much deeper than the thoughts of the human mind. Edwards believed that the affections were the source of true religion.

He asserted that all human feeling, thinking, and acting were rooted in the affections, the underlying loves and dispositions that incline us toward or from things. He believed that religion must influence and spring from these deepest levels of the human psyche. The Scriptures confirm believers' hearts in the affections: fear, joy, hope, love, hatred, desire, sorrow, gratitude, compassion, and zeal.

Edwards's genius compassion and sincerity had made the Great Awakening movement a real revival.

The Blessing of Whitefield's Ministry to the Colonies

During Whitefield's seven trips to the colonies, thousands showed up wherever he preached with his magical style anointed by the Holy Spirit. During his preaching career, Whitefield was the frontrunner of open-air preaching. This special way was the key to reaching out to thousands of larger farms off the main transportation routes; this was a special ministry no other preachers before him had performed.

Pulpit Presentation of Whitefield

The traditional style of preaching had been defined by medieval and classical oration. The preacher's craft was aimed at injecting learning into discourse in such a way that the mind would be filled with information and heart filled with the truths of Scripture.

Whitefield's unique genius style had been inspired by his childhood experiences on the stage.

> In terms of the presentation of himself in the pulpit, Whitefield would call "talking heads": preachers whose embodied self was generally hidden from the congregation by robes, elevated pulpits, and scripts, and whose motions were limited largely to hand movements punctuating the doctrines of the sermon. Speakers and hearer were fixed within the physical space of the church. University and church were the only two places where knowledge was transmitted.

Summary of Chapter 4
Whitfield

- Whitfield made seven trips to the colonies.
- He and Edwards were catalysts of the Great Awakening.
- Whitefield knew Edwards (1703–1758), Theodore J. Frelinghuysen (1691–1748), and William Tennent (1673–1746).
- Whitefield was befriended and admired by Benjamin Franklin.

Edwards

- grandson of Solomon Stoddard
- knew Hebrew, Greek, and Latin when he entered Yale at age thirteen
- became pastor in Northampton, Massachusetts, where God started the Great Awakening

- served as missionary to Native Americans after being released from his church
- became president of the College of New Jersey (now Princeton) in 1758
- was possibly the greatest theologian America ever produced
- died of a smallpox inoculation

Whitfield's Marvelous Talents

Whitefield proved to be a master of self-promotion before the age of modern mass media. He built his refreshing revivalist spirit around the traditional institutional supports in the established or nonconforming churches and press. With the assistance of weekly newspapers and magazines, Whitefield rode the rising tides of a dawning age of commerce and marketing into a growing mass-media revolution.

Was the Awakening Movement God's Mandate or a Man-Made Religious Movement?

For decades, many scholars argued about the nature of the Great Awakening, but no one could argue about its impact on church and society. The revivals had a lasting impact on American Christianity; the authority of the church was changed by the appearance of lay preachers who were unattached to established churches. The breakdown of a traditional clerical elite system shook the foundations of the old religious culture and changed the social order into a popular movement with a direct appeal to the masses.

In the Wake of the Great Awakening

> According to Eera Stiles, president of Yale College after the awakening,

The first major result of the Awakening, the Congregationalists of New England received the greatest benefit. The establishment of the new Congregational church was over 150 since 1740. The Awakening brought total number of Congregational Church to 530. Historians have estimated that from 25,000 to 50,000 people were added to the membership of New England church as a result of the Great Awakening.

Spiritual revival led to dramatic social changes as it brought a renewed interest in religious matters or duties. From the historians' perspective, whatever the results of the arguments were is not important. The important thing is that nobody could ignore or deny the lasting impacts the Great Awakening produced.

The Influence of Whitefield's Preaching

Whitefield was the most influential giant and preacher of the Great Awakening; Edwards was the most important apologist of that era.

Mass Media's Coverage of the Awakening Movement

Benjamin Franklin knew Whitefield and printed his sermons and journals; he held Whitfield in high regard despite their different religious views. Franklin fell under the grand itinerant's spell when Whitefield visited him at Philadelphia seeking funds and supplies for the orphanage he founded in Georgia. Franklin accommodated Whitefield at his home, profited monetarily from publishing Whitefield's writings, and corresponded with him for more than thirty years.

One biographer has counted forty-five descriptions of Whitefield's preaching in the weekly issues of Franklin's *Gazette* as well as eight front pages that included texts of Whitefield's sermons. Whitefield's ability to personify the awakening movement made the friendly public medias a channel by which he could reach countless readers even before his arrival at the next preaching destination.

As proof that a revival of religion was due in the colonies and that existing churches were not providing what people wanted, the Great Awakening began almost simultaneously in three colonies: Rev. Theodore Frelinghuysen started a revival in Raritan Valley, New Jersey; Rev. William Tennent began the Long College for revivalists at Neshaminy, Pennsylvania; and Edwards began his famous imprecatory sermon in Northampton, Connecticut.

> The net result of the Awakening in terms of pure religion is impossible to estimate; in term of sociology it is more palpable. It brought more people into the Protestant churches, but split them up, setting congregations against their ministers, and reviving intolerance. Connecticut, for instance, repealed its toleration act in 1743. Once ignorant and emotional people had tasted the strong drink of revivalism they cared no more for traditional worship; new congregations were formed, some of which died out after a few years, while others became Baptist, Methodists, or "New Light" Presbyterian. Calmer souls sought refuge in the Anglican churches or Quaker meetings, which were the least affected by the Awakening.

Chapter 5

LEGACIES OF EDWARDS'S AND WHITEFIELD'S TESTIMONIES

The Divine Duty of Preachers to Proclaim the Gospel

Our Lord sends forth His disciples to proclaim the gospel.

> To open their eyes, *in order to turn them* from darkness to light and *from* the power of Satan to God, that they may receive forgiveness of sins and an inheritance among those who are sanctified by faith in Me. (Acts 26:18)

Preachers Testify That Jesus Is the Savior of the World

The apostle John gave us an infallible declaration of our Savior's mission: "We have seen and do testify that the Father sent the Son to be the Savior of the world" (John 3:11–21).

Preachers answered God's call and took the gospel, received the conviction of truth, and went to the fields proclaiming to the people what had been unheard there. Faithful servants of God are obligated to carry their duty of preaching the gospel according to 2 Timothy 4:2: "Preach the word! Be ready in season and out of season; rebuke, exhort, with all long suffering and teaching."

We witnessed Edwards's and Whitefield's whole lives and their ministries in the awakening era to fulfill that command and duty from God. They preached the Word of God faithfully as they served the Lord.

The Trumpets: (Numbers 10:9)—Feast of Trumpets

This feast of trumpets reminds the chosen people of their covenant and puts God in remembrance of His promise. To us, these trumpets would have great measures of grace. We must also rouse all our strength and aspirations and cry fervently with trumpet voice to God.

The Farmers: (Matthew 13:1–9)—Parable of the Sower

The duty of priests is to proclaim the good news of agape love to plant seeds in the humble hearts of listeners.

The Shining Lights: (Matthew 5:16)—Believers Are Light

"Let your light so shine before men, that they may see your good works and glorify your Father in heaven."

The Watchmen: (Zechariah 11:11)—Prophecy of the Shepherds

In the tribulation resulting from the breaking of that covenant of favor, the poor of the flock, the godly remnant, recognized the fulfillment of God's work.

In Ephesians 4:11–12, God gave spiritual gifts to the apostles, prophets, evangelists, pastors, and teachers "for the equipping of the saints for the work of ministry, for the edifying of the body of Christ."

Edwards and Whitefield followed the divine calling, preached the gospel of repentance, and paved the road for the harvest of the Lord. They were not afraid to condemn those who taught falsehoods. They were faithful and hard working in admonishing and reproving in season whenever and wherever they visited.

> Edwards used noble images drawn from the scripture to illustrate the premier significance of preachers in the work of redemption. They are like the trumpets blown by Old Testament priests at the great Jewish feasts, like farmers who go forth to sow seed in the earth (Mt. 13:1–9), like burning and shining lights (John 5:25) and like mirrors that convey and reflect beams of the light of the world. When they preach the gospel rightly, they are the very "voice of the great God." Using earthier comparisons, he compared them to Samson's jawbone of the ass (Jdg. 15:14–16), teeth that a nurse uses to chew food for babies, saliva (spit) that Jesus used to mix with dirt and open the eyes of a blind man (John 9:6–7), David's sling that helped kill Goliath (1 Sam. 17:49), and ox that treads out the corn (1 Cor. 9:9–10).

> Dr. A.V.G. Allen of early eighteenth century was Edwards's biographer and critic, and a careful student of his unpublished, as well as of his published, writings, says "He was at his best and greatest, most original and creative, when he described the divine love." Such passages as the following show this quality: "When we behold the fragrant rose and lily, we see His love and purity. So the green trees and fields and singing of birds are the emanations of His infinite joy and benignity. The easiness and naturalness of trees and vines are shadows of His beauty and loveliness." Edwards's favorite text was,

"I am the rose of Sharon and Lily of the valleys," and his favorite words were "sweet and bright."

In Edwards's essay "Surprising Work of God," he wrote,

God has seemed to have gone out His usual way, in the quickness of His **work**, and the swift progress His Spirit has made in His **operation** on the hearts of many. It is wonderful that persons should be so suddenly and yet so greatly changed. Many have been taken from a **loose** and careless way of **living**, and seized with strong convictions of their guilt and misery, and in very **time** old things have passed away, and all things have new with them.

Edwards wrote,

The drift of the Spirit of **God** in His **legal** strivings with persons has seemed most evidently to be, to bring to a **conviction** of their absolute dependence on His sovereign **power** and grace, and a universal necessity of a mediator. This has been effected by leading them more and more to a sense of their exceeding wickedness and guiltiness in His sight; their pollution, and the insufficiency of their own righteousness; that they can in no wise help themselves, and that **God** would be wholly just and righteous in rejecting them and all that they do, and in casting them off forever." "Persons after their conversion often speak of **religious** things as seeming new to them; that preaching is a new thing; that it seems to them they never heard preaching before; that Bible is a new book; they find there new chapters, new psalms, new histories, because they see them in a new **light**. Here was a remarkable instance of an aged woman, of about seventy years, who had spent most of her days under Mr. Stoddard's powerful **ministry**. **Reading** in the New Testament concerning Christ's sufferings for **sinners**, she seemed to be astonished at what she read, as what was real and very wonderful, but quite new to her. At first, before she had time to turn her thoughts, she thought she had often heard of it, and read it, but never till now saw it was real. She then cast in her mind how wonderful this was that the Son of God should undergo such things for sinners, and how she had spent her time in ungratefully sinning against so good a God, and such a Savior; though she was a person, apparently, of a very blameless and inoffensive life. And she was overcome by those considerations that her nature was ready to fail under them: those who were about her, and knew not what was the matter, were surprised, and thought she was dying.

George Whitefield: The Matchless Winner of Souls for God

Charles Wesley wrote an elegy for Whitefield in 1770.

Though long by following multitudes admired, No party for himself he e'er desired;

His one desire to make the Saviour known, To magnify the name of Christ alone:

If others strove who should the greatest be, No lover of preeminence was he,

Nor envied those his Lord vouchsafed to bless, But joyed in theirs as in his own success.

John Greenleaf Whittier, the American Quaker poet, lived not far from Newburyport, Massachusetts. He commemorated Whitefield in his poem "The Preacher," in which he wrote,

> Long shall the traveler strain his eye
>
> From the railroad car as it passes by,
>
> And the vanishing town behind him search
>
> For the slender spirit of the Whitefield Church,
>
> And feel the one moment the ghosts of trade,
>
> And fashion and folly and pleasure laid,
>
> By the thought of that life of pure intent,
>
> That voice of warning yet eloquent,
>
> Of one on the errands of angel sent.
>
> And if, where he labored, the flood of sins,
>
> Like the tide from the harbor bar set in,
>
> And over a life of time and sense,
>
> The church spires lifted their vain defense …
>
> Still, as the gem in its civic crown,
>
> Precious beyond the world's renowned,
>
> His memory hallows that ancient town.

Whitefield's popularity outweighed his critics. In the course of his many preaching tours in England, Wales, Scotland, Ireland, and North America he preached approximately eighteen thousand sermons. He preached his final sermon in Exeter, New Hampshire, on September 29, 1770.

The Characteristics of the Two Great Evangelists

Compared with the preachers' duties from above, I found that Edwards and Whitefield fulfilled all four duties. They were the divine anointed preachers who arrived at the era of the Great Awakening and dedicated their lives to serving the Lord diligently. Apart from that, their exceptional characters had an invaluable impact on the revivals.

Compassionate Hearts

Edwards and Whitefield were converted at very young ages, and they had compassionate hearts. At Oxford, Whitefield prayed three times a day and fasted once a week; he was influenced by Henry Scougal's *The life of God in the Soul of Man*, which taught him that all must be born again or be damned.

They answered the divine calling to serve the Lord in different functions and roles. Whitefield fulfilled the role of the most important preacher of the Great Awakening while Edwards fulfilled the role as the most important apologist.

As Whitefield defended his faithful walk in preaching, Edwards defended his belief and faith in writing.

The leading theologian, Edwards, and the major orator, Whitefield, set the values that united the revivalists. They motivated the church people and the general public with enthusiastic spirits and paved the way to a resounding chapter in the spiritual revival of the colonies.

With the rare exception of the disagreement between Edwards and Whitefield on the subject of bodily manifestations,

> George Whitefield and Charles Wesley generally viewed the bodily manifestation as distractions and interferences to the main business of preaching

> the word. In Edwards's case, we know that he preached at services that included exuberant bodily manifestations. Yet there is no indication that he ever encouraged such manifestations. Theologically speaking, he viewed them as equivocal in character, and so a direct encouragement of this manifestation- such as Cennick attributed to Wesley-might lead people mistakenly to identify these outward phenomena with the Spirit's inward work ... It should be noted that Wesley drew boundaries with regard to acceptable bodily manifestations.

Edwards's and Whitefield's lives demonstrated moral integrity as well as spiritual strength through their sermons. Their influence was not without controversy.

The criticism that they stirred up audiences with accounts of human sinfulness and the horrors of hell intensified the religious life of colonial church people.

Whitefield surprised everyone at his peak of popularity in England and went to Georgia briefly as a missionary in February 1738. He returned to England and took priest's orders from the Church of England. He collected money by his personal influence with upper-class friends to build an orphanage in Georgia.

> Its spiritual and cultural influence upon the religious and social life of the country was profound: especially missionary, educational, and humanitarian activities were greatly stimulated. Only recently have we begun to understand this contribution in its full significance. Yet this movement did not produce many distinctly new types of organizations. That is partly due to the insistence upon personal experience which is characteristic of all revivalism. This emphasis explains the tendency to extreme

expressions of emotionalism which some of its students-historians and psychologists have regarded as typical of revival religion in general.

The conflict started between the New Learning, the unprecedented, radical waves that hit churches' traditional systems and challenged the clergies' spiritual qualifications with the intense religious enthusiasm ushered in by the Great Awakening.

The phenomenon of "enthusiasm" once more made an appearance, generating concern within the church over its apparent excesses, Edwards himself was concerned that such seemingly hysterical behavior could bring the church into disrepute and even destabilize the social order. Confronted with obvious evidence of ecstatic religious experiences, however, Edwards began to develop what we might now call a "psychology of religion"-an attempt to understand and make sense of ecstatic phenomena as natural responses to a sense of guilt or the realization of forgiveness. His 1741 commencement address at Yale, entitled *"The Distinguishing Marks of a Work of the Spirit of God,* sought to distinguish between a primary divine inspiration and a secondary human response. The latter (but not the former), he argued, could be understood in naturalist terms.

Zealous Desire for Missionary Work

Whitefield first visited Georgia in 1738 and revisited it in 1740; he followed the footsteps of John and Charles Wesley as they labored separately in Savannah and St. Simon's Island since 1736 without much satisfaction.

Whitefield had very high and positive hope for the orphanage in Savannah, "because the longer I continued there, the larger the congregations grew, and I rarely knew a night ... when the house was not full."

Cornelius Winter was at Whitefield's orphanage when he learned of the evangelist's death. His report [5]:

> You have no conception of the effect of Mr. Whitefield's death upon the inhabitations of the province of Georgia. All the black cloth in the store was brought up; the pulpit and the desk of church, the branches, the organ loft, the pews of the governor and council, were covered with black. The governor and council in deep mourning, convened at the state-house, and went in procession to church, and were received by the organ playing a funeral dirge. In his funeral sermon for Whitefield, John Wesley asked, *"Have we read or heard of any person since the apostles, who ... called so many thousand, so many myraids of sinners to repentance?*

Whitefield was indeed a great honor and testimony to our Lord.

Edwards also went to the frontier settlement of Stockbridge in the Berkshire Hills after he left his ministry of Southampton, Connecticut. He went with his wife and eight children to minister to a small Indian reservation. It turned out to be the blessings that Edwards found leisure to write *The Nature of True Virtue, Original Sin, and Freedom of the Will*, which combined with his earlier treatise on religious affections, dedicated his effort to continue his study of the theology of Calvinism.

Joyful Hearts in Serving the Lord

Edwards and Whitefield shared the joy of their personal religious conversion experiences. To Edwards, conversion was a profound emotional experience in addition to an intellectual experience.

The awakening movement did not produce too many new types of religious organizations. Instead, the characteristic revivalism marked by Edwards's and Whitefield's spiritual walks was hard to wipe off. The truth Edwards insisted on was that the Spirit must penetrate the surface convictions of human reason to awaken a "sense of heart" focused on the glory of the Lord.

The Unique Virtue of True Followers of Christ

Edwards believed,

Virtue is love to intelligent being in general. But God has infinitely the greatest share of existence; he is infinitely the great being, so true virtue must essentially and radically consist in supreme love to God." Such true virtue cannot be found through reason and understanding for it is of the affections and the disposition; it arises from the ascendancy of the supreme passion, love over self-love.

Whitefield wrote on August 3, 1739, "I am no friend to sinless perfection. I believed the existence (though not the dominion) of sin remains in the hearts of the greatest believers."

Edwards stood at the center of the Great Awakening among his revivalist peers; that had to do with his *Nature of True Virtue*, which was a work of philosophy instead of theology. He taught rightly in The *Nature of True Virtue* and warned of the idolatry that led to demonization.

Edwards equated the moral sense with the remnants of natural conscience in fallen humankind. Conscience had its use, to be sure; it had been implanted by God to foster peace in civil society. But it was not part of the true virtue, which proceeded only from regeneration and encompassed the love of all creation. True virtue, in Edwards's view, was composed of love of all being-not just of oneself, or one's family or community or nation, such as one found in natural morality. A principle of love so complete, he contends, was attainable only through grace and religious conversion.

The Practice of Great Love of God's Reconciliation

Edwards and Whitefield served for the glory of God. As 1 Peter 4:8 commands, "And above all things have fervent love for one another, for love will cover a multitude of sins."

Edwards always believed that his Christian duty to love others flowed out of his fervent love of God. He knew that true, biblical love runs much deeper, that it came naturally from the love of God that extends to others. There can be no growth in godliness without the practice of love.

Whitefield's moral integrity was admirable; he was generous with his caring for the spiritual state of Harvard College. At Harvard, it was reported, "The College is entirely changed; the students are full of God." Yet Harvard's leading professors later wrote a fifteen-page pamphlet denouncing Whitefield in a reply to Whitefield's denunciation of Harvard's spiritual state. Whitefield was not moved from his firm view. The confrontation between Whitefield and Harvard didn't last long, and it had a happy ending. After Whitefield learned that Harvard's library burned in 1764, he gave books and raised money for a new library. The president and fellows of Harvard voted Whitefield a gratitude of thanks. What a character and great integrity that Whitefield showed us all!

Their Sermons Were Faithful to the Biblical Truth of God

The apostle Paul pointed out in 1 Thessalonians 2:4, "But as we have been approved by God to be entrusted with the **Gospel**, so we speak, not as pleasing man, but God who tests our hearts."

Example of Edwards's Sermon

The main point of "The Torments of the Wicked in Hell, No Occasion of the Saints in Heaven" (Revelation 18:20) came from 2 Peter 2:4, "Cast them down to hell, deliver them into the chains of darkness"

> But Now, when he shall be suffered to deceive the nations no more, his kingdom will be confined to hell. In this test is contained part of what John heard uttered upon? This occasion; and in these words we may observe:
>
> 1). To whom this voice is directed, *viz. to the holy prophets and apostles*, and the rest of inhabitants, of the heavenly world. When God shall pour out his wrath upon the antichristian church, it will be seen, and taken notice of, by all the inhabitants of heaven, even by holy prophets and apostles. Neither will they see as unconcerned spectators.
>
> 2). What they are called upon by the voice to do, *viz. to rejoice over Babylon* now destroyed, and lying under the wrath of God. They are not directed to rejoice over her in prosperity, but in flames, and behold the smoke of her burning ascending up for ever and ever.
>
> 3). A reason given: for God *hath avenged* you on her;

i.e. God has executed just vengeance upon her, for shedding your blood, and cruelly persecuting you. For thus the matter is represented, that antichrist had been guilty for shedding the blood of holy prophets and apostles; but he had shed the blood of those who were their followers, who were of the same spirit, and of the same church, and same mystical body. The prophets and apostles in heaven are nearly related and united to the saints on earth; they live, as it were, in true Christians in all ages. So that by slaying these, persecutors show that they would slay the prophets and apostles, if they would; and they indeed do it as much as in them lies.

On the same account, Christ says of Jews in his time Luke 11:50, "that the blood of all the prophets, which was shed from the foundation of the world, may be required of this generation, from the blood of Abel, unto the blood of Zacharias, which perished between the altar and temple: verily I say unto you, it shall required of this generation." So Christ himself is said to have been crucified in the antichrist church, Rev.11:8. "And their dead bodies shall lie in the great city, which spiritually is called Sodom and Egypt, where also our lord was crucified.

So all the inhabitants of heaven, all the saints from the beginning of the world, and the angels also, are called upon to rejoice over Babylon, because of God's vengeance upon her, wherein he avenges them: all of them had in effect been injured and persecuted by antichrist. Indeed they are not too called upon to rejoice in having their revenge glutted, but in seeing justice executed and in seeing love and tenderness of God towards them is manifested in his severity towards their enemies.

Edwards continued,

When the saints in glory shall see the wrath of God executed on ungodly men, it will be no occasion of grief on them, but rejoicing. It is not only the sight of God's wrath executed on those wicked men who are of the antichrist church, which will be an occasion of rejoicing of the saints in glory, but also the sight of the destruction of all God's enemies: whether they have been the followers of antichrist or not, that alter not the case, if they have been the enemies of God, and of Jesus Christ. All wicked men will at least be destroyed together, as being united in the same cause and interest, as being all Satan's army. They will stand together at the day of judgment, as being all of the same company.

Edwards followed the biblical truth to warn churches,

The things they are called upon to rejoice at, is the execution of God's wrath upon his and their enemies. And if it be matter of rejoicing to them to see justice executed in part upon them, or to see the beginning of the execution of it in this world, for the same reason will they rejoice with greater joy, in beholding fully executed. For the thing here mentioned as the foundation of their joy, is the execution of just vengeance: *Rejoice, for God hath avenged you on her.*

Edwards's sermon ended with two resounding propositions

> Prop 1: The glorified saints will see the wrath of God executed upon the ungodly men. Prop 2: The saints in heaven possess all things as their own, therefore all things contribute to their joy and happiness.

> Like most Puritans, Edwards preached from the Bible, dividing his sermons into three sections- "Text," "Doctrine," and "Application"—each saturated with Scripture. Even his own phrasing was often strikingly biblical. He chose words carefully for the images they created in the minds of his hearers.

Whitefield visited Northampton in 1740; he stayed with Edwards and preached at church. Edwards reported,

> The congregation was extraordinarily melting ... almost the whole assembly being in tears for a great part of the time." It was after that visit that Edwards preached his famous sermon "Sinners in the hands of an angry God.

Sarah Edwards observed that Whitefield aimed more at affecting the heart by proclaiming the simple truths of the Bible than any other preacher she had heard.

The Debate between the "New Spirit" and the "Old Spirit"

Before the awakening, Anglicanism and Quakerism had broken the dominant barrier with the Congregational denomination. The God-sent new form of acts was informal or even very special gatherings that had spread out by Whitefield's open-air gatherings. They were so blessed in Spirit that they were like a new style of preaching.

> The collective protest of the Awakening movements

led certain individuals and groups into secession. That, however, was more exception than the rule. The vehement controversies over the character and value of the revival movements (particularly over the extraordinary exercises accompanying them), which continued for so long after they subsided, shows that, even if separation did not occur to any considerable extent, the question of limit of the orthodox and heterodox, the permitted and the illicit, was definitely put and eagerly discussed in the various denominations affected by the revival (Baptists, Methodists, Presbyterians). As we know that emotional starvation is one of the causes which produce sectarianism, we understand how close to secession many groups and individuals in the revival movements actually were.

The Peak of the Awakening Era

Edwards himself was witness to such events in Northampton during the winter of 1734–35. The final weeks of 1734 witnessed conversions, "very remarkable and suddenly, one after another." The revival continued into the New Year, reaching its peak during March and April 1735. There was hardly a household in the town that was not affected. Perhaps as many as three hundred individuals, "about the same numbers of males as females," appeared to have been converted. *Edwards* began to develop what we might now call a "psychology of religion"-an attempt to understand and make sense of ecstatic phenomena as natural responses to a sense of guilt or realization of forgiveness. His 1741 commencement address at Yale, entitled *"The*

Distinguishing Marks of a Work of the Spirit of God," sought to distinguish between a primary divine inspiration and a secondary human response. The latter (but not the former), he argued, could be understood in naturalist terms.

This was the incident at the peak of revival involved Whitefield.

At the peak of the revival, its rhetoric took on an anti-intellectual tone. Whitefield, upon visiting Harvard, criticized the institution for teaching such secular and moralist writers as Tillotson and Samuel Clark rather than evangelical writers. Gilbert Tennent described those studies as "mere critics" and Davenport staged a massive book burning at New London, which included works not only by Tilllotson but even by Boston's Benjamin Coleman, combined his Latitudinarian sentiments with warm support for the revival. Davenport was extreme; most of the prominent revivalists were not in fact anti-intellectual at all in spite of their heated rhetoric. Many were firm supporters of education. The New Side Presbyterian minister William Tennent had set up an instructional school for ministers at the "Log College," where their graduates in turn set up academics of their own, including Samuel Blair, Robert Smith, and Samuel Finley.

The Awakening was a great impetus to the creation of educational institutions in America, and the origins of both the College of New Jersey (today's Princeton) and the New Hampshire College that became Dartmouth can be traced to the revival.

The Relationship between Religious Revivalism and the Great Awakening

The revival movement in eighteenth-century colonial America was a form of social change that started with religious reform and led to revitalization. The movement was a process that turned demoralization into revitalization. The key element was the attitude of the people involved in that society. As more people responded to the pressure to follow a new direction, steps were taken to restructure and reorganize.

Scriptures' Command of the Preachers' Calling from God

The apostle Paul explained this issue very well in Philemon 1:6: "That the communication of thy faith may become effectual by the acknowledging of every good thing which is in you in Christ Jesus." Paul went further in Philemon 2:13; he wrote that every good thing was the result of the fact that "it is God which works in your both to will and to do his good pleasure."

Paul meant to secure proper recognition from others of the existence of faith in our hearts that would let others see we are truly pious and understand to what extent we have faith. Calvin believed that the apostle here did not proceed in the commendation of Philemon but rather expressed what he desired for him from the Lord.

Preachers are obligated to the Lord's calling to proclaim the gospel of the salvation and to remind people to repent for the kingdom of God is at hand.

The awakening's architects believed God was grieving for the sins of people in general.

They pursued a divine solution to correct the deteriorated moral situation. This solution was based on their belief that by acknowledging and proclaiming the urgent need for a new pattern of rebirth, people would return to God. This new pattern suggested that people needed to turn from their old spiritual status of sinners and become newborn and righteous in God's eyes.

People undergo conversion by the influence of divine grace; their new life patterns are changed; their contrite hearts would confirm a new pattern of spiritual being; their prior sinful nature was working under the power of divine grace that began a new way of behavior.

First, there were more people seeking opportunities to join others in Bible study and church meeting and fellowship. Second, there were more people recognizing the call to serve others and teach and preach the gospel, and more people were eager to encourage the spiritual growth of new converts.

Leaders of the movement such as Edwards promoted the establishment of a church that supported schools in training people for ministry. As a result, denominational colleges such as Princeton, Brown, and Dartmouth were founded to serve that need. This form of social action began with institutional reforms; it was led by William Tennent's deep vision, faith, and commitment to teaching youth at the Log College (1735), and it had proven that the evangelists had responded faithfully to the Great Commission.

The Testimonies of the Preachers of the Great Awakening

The revival took a great toll on Edwards's ministry. He tried very hard to distinguish between the converted and the unconverted, and that eventually led him to renege on Stoddardeanism, his grandfather's practice of allowing anyone to partake of Holy Communion, not merely the regenerate.

I compared the propositions of the Great Awakening to Scripture.

Signs Accompanying a Counterfeit Revival

- It preachers too much on God's wrath.
- Its professed converts later fall into scandal.
- It stirs audiences' imaginations.
- It prompts too much attention.
- It produces too strong effects on the bodies of the believers.
- It is promoted too much by influences of example and testimony.

Signs Accompanying a Genuine Revival

Isaiah 35:3 reads, "Strengthen you the weak hands and confirm the feeble knees." As the Holy Spirit moved, it made revival work. The people shall witness the work of the Spirit.

- God and the Holy Spirit lead hearers to desire Jesus.
- It will lead people (including the priests) to confess their sins and be holy.
- It makes people love the Bible more.
- It enhances believers' faith.
- It motivates people to love and serve God and evangelize others.

Psalm 32:5 reads, "I acknowledged my sin unto thee, and mine iniquity has I not hid: I said, I will confess my transgressions unto the Lord; and thou forgives the iniquity of my sin."

The confession of sin to God necessarily involves acknowledgment of Him as God, who should be honored in worship and served. Jude 12 warns priests and false teachers, "These are hidden reels at your love feasts, as they feast with you without fear, shepherds feeding themselves; fruitless trees in late autumn, twice dead, uprooted." The awakening movement raised the issue of the spiritual holiness of the churches' priests and had also encouraged laypeople to participate in church.

The Work of the Holy Spirit in Revivals

John 16:8 reads, "When he comes, he will convict the world of guilt in regard to sin and righteousness and judgment." The Holy Spirit has a twofold office directed at the world and believers to convince the whole world. He who is convinced of sin either accepts the righteousness of Christ or is judged with Satan.

While humanity seeks after self-righteousness, God is seeking their hearts. Jesus promised the children of God in Matthew 18:20, "For where two or three come together in my name, there am I with them."

The corporate (massive gathering) prayers were the evidence of the Holy Spirit and a prerequisite for any outpourings of the Holy Spirit. Edwards believed that corporate prayer was the key factor in igniting the awakening movement.

As the Great Awakening went on, God rose up many strong leaders to guide its progress. Edwards was the powerful orator; he was able to move audiences deeply with his sermons. Whitefield's open-air meetings reached out to thousands of people who did not have access to churches. He was indeed God-sent to bless the people from rural areas and slaves to receive the gospel for the first time in the colonies' history.

The preachers of the Great Awakening were very focused on the Reformation's doctrine of justification by faith and atonement; they seemed also to emphasize God's judgment and grace. Prior to any spiritual revival were the assumptions that the current spiritual condition of society was in decline and that there was an urgent need to correct that decline.

The growth of religious toleration was paralleled by a decline in the authority of the established churches, which faced a losing battle with its congregational members. For quite a long period before the mid-eighteenth century, the clergy could not contain its churches' members; those members were always free to leave.

Beyond a doubt, one of the principal causes of the decline of the Puritan theocracy was the fact that a large area of unoccupied land was available to the colonies' inhabitants. Similarly, in Virginia, the Anglican Church was unable to keep pace with the westward movement of its communicants. An increasing number of Virginians took religion with decreasing seriousness, and there were many who went to church only as a matter of form or for social reasons. The colony's clergy repeatedly complained but apparently in vain about those who desecrated the Sabbath by drinking, fighting, swearing, and dancing.

The ideas of the Enlightenment developed first in the field of science. By the same token, the development of new social and cultural movements had divided many Christians. On the other hand, Protestantism took a different aspect facing the issue of the Enlightenment; part of the reason might be due to the lack of a single, dominant concept of how to bind believers together.

Edwards and Whitefield—Major Catalysts of the Great Awakening

The seeds of the awakening were sown in 1734, when Edwards began to preach revivalist sermons in Northampton. Edwards was an exceptional thinker in the realms of theology and philosophy. He set the Christian theological foundation of the awakening with his writings and sermons. His impact was undeniable in spite of his controversial positions on baptism of church membership.

The Great Awakening had a lasting influence on American Christianity. Many of the converts of that time had life-changing experiences at spiritual revivals.

Whitefield was the key figure who fanned the flames of revival and spread them across the northeastern colonies.

John Wesley Confirmed Edwards's Classic Writing

Edwards's classic *A Faithful Narrative of the Surprising Work of God* drew international attention to the awakening; between 1737 and 1739, this book went through three editions and twenty printings. It helped inspire Whitefield and others when it was reprinted in London and Edinburgh and even translated into Dutch and German in 1737.

> When John Wesley read this classic writings afoot between London and Oxford, He said, *"surely this is the Lord's doing,"* Wesley wrote in his journal; presently he began to obtain the same effects with his own preaching, and in little while the Methodist Church was born. Whitefield, an eloquent young minister sent out to Georgia by the trustees, read *A Faithful Narration pamphlet in Savannah*, and his amazing career as a revivalist dates from that hour.

The Division of the Great Awakening

Edwards, an emotional preacher, emphasized the absolute power of God. His most famous sermon, the harrowing "Sinners in the Hands of an Angry God," compared sinners to spiders dangled over a flame. He believed based on his personal experience in an effective and sensible way that went beyond the rational; he experienced the glory of God in his heart.

He was fearless in the pulpit; he never hesitated to preach against sin. He denounced churches' policies of reserving front seats for the wealthy.

On the one hand, Edwards defended the religion

of the heart against the critics of revival who condemned emotionalism to the point that they were left with a religion of the head. But Edwards also denounced religion that was merely emotional, devoid of cognitive understanding of basic Christian truth. In a manner unmatched by most other spiritual theologians, Edwards linked head and heart, experience and understanding.

What made Edwards stand out from his peers was his confidence and conviction of "the total man of heart and mind." Edwards believed it was impossible to separate heart and mind when dealing with religious issues. He believed that when a person was moved by the Spirit of God, he or she would have a profoundly emotional experience. There are three elements: a person's will, custom, and reason that determined the outcome.

> Yes, all these things, but above all, it is his whole past life, all his desires, that which he wants most of all. "Only when God's Spirit shows man the true aim of his desires and grants him a new heart and will, only then can man turn to God."

While other religious leaders in the Awakening who rejected of Edwards and the resulting divorce between reason and religion was an example of rejecting the original spirit of Puritanism. Chauncy and his followers went their separate ways, stressing cold, hard morality, apart from a warm piety; this was to culminate in Unitarianism.

At the peak of the awakening in 1741, Rev. William Cooper, a well-known preacher in Boston, said,

> The golden showers have been restrained; few sons

have been born to God; and the hearts of Christians not so quickened, warmed and refreshed under the ordinances, as they have been ... But now, the Lord whom we have sought has suddenly come to his temple. The dispensations of grace we are now under are certainly such as neither we nor our fathers have seen; and in some circumstances so wonderful, that I believe there has not been the like since the extraordinary pouring out of the Spirit immediately after our Lord's ascension ... The apostolically times seem to have returned upon us.

The Overall Effects of the Great Awakening

No one can ignore the social effects of the awakening movement. It elevated the common people by advocating the self-authenticating religious experience, which freed them from religious autocracy. Lay servants emerged to challenge the barriers of the church's aged and strict qualification rules involving ministering. The New Lights accused the Old Lights of lacking the inner spiritual strength. This trend encouraged new members to actively participate in church programs. That was the key to becoming a mandate for early social action since part of obeying Christ is to help those outside the churches. It accelerated the splintering of American Protestantism; it stimulated the divisions in existing denominations and the growth of new groups. For example, Congregationalists and Presbyterians were split into supporters and opponents of the new spiritual group. It also weakened the traditional structure of church authority in colonial society. The revivals encouraged converted laypeople to question and then judge their ministers' spiritual qualifications.

The effects of the revivals were phenomenal. Statistics are hard to find, but we know that at least 150 new Congregational churches were established in a twenty-year period and 30,000 more between 1740 and 1742 [6], almost doubling the number before the awakening. The signs of moral results were also very noticeable—nine Christian colleges and universities were established in the colonies.

In 1743, Boston's Thomas Prince started a magazine, Christian History, whose sole purpose was to stoke revivals by reporting on revivals.

> How much it was based on wishful thinking, credulity, or sheer invention is moot since most of the details about revivals originated with their preachers and press agents. But it tells that Edwards was turned out of his own church when the frenzy finally abated. While "there was a glorious work of God wrought," he surmised in 1751, "false appearance and counterfeits" did their work as well, such that "the number of true converts was not as great as was then imagined.

In reviewing church history of the awakening movement, the English and American evangelists shared similar ideologies in terms of political and social reform and were blamed for their failure to bring about the overall churches' reform.

New Church Forms after the Revivals

The wind of evangelical spirit spread throughout the colonies; the evangelical meant "Protestant" to all. England's Christians were influenced by the Great Awakening; they called the movement the "evangelical party." Many traditional church ministers witnessed Whitefield's preaching as the work of God and tried to follow his model. Other ministers were disturbed by the difficulty unschooled

---

6   Tony Cauchi. "The First Worldwide Awakening of 1725." http://www.revival-library.org/index.php/catalogues-menu/1725.

adults would have in understanding their preaching.

The gospel is the power of God, and its truth was manifested clearly through the true preaching in the awakening era. As a result of the renewal of revivalism, many first-time listeners had the opportunity to listen to the gospel, and many even joined the new churches. The awakening emphasized the importance of Christians' inner religious experiences; it also strengthened the dissenting churches—Presbyterian, Baptist, and Methodist.

Edwards was a witness in the winter of 1734–35 to many conversions in Northampton, "very remarkably and suddenly, one after another" according to him. The revival continued into the new year, reaching its peak during March and April 1735.

The efforts from the enthusiastic preaching that had swept over the colonies had the impact on the awakening movement that reached disadvantaged people and rural farms' slavers. Urged into action by the Great Awakening of the 1740s, white evangelical Protestants began proselytizing black Americans; the most successful at this were the Methodists.

The spiritual revival movement made a widespread impact across the colonies, and within a few decades, Christian values generated tremendous effects on churches as well as society.

The Division of Churches

After the revival, the colonies' churches transformed into a new form or spirit; the revival also served as symbol of a melting pot, giving immigrant communities more contact with other colonies. It made different denominational churches such as the members of Presbyterian congregations and Dutch-educated immigrants identify themselves as Americans.

In the New England region, the Presbyterians and Dutch Reformed had cracked under the impact of the awakening. The divisions started in the 1740s; both denominations dealt with the schisms and were transformed into more-egalitarian and pietistic organizations; there were less formal conceptions of the church. However, Christianity in New England was characterized by two significant messages: the biblical supremacy and the sacred relationship between God and believers. This region was particularly blessed by its tradition of evangelicalism, purity of theological doctrine, and the spirit of pursuit in the service of reform.

In the Middle Region

Parting from the churches' style of old England, the revivals fragmented churches' members from British, German, Dutch, and other backgrounds into an inherited unity that witnessed the emergence of a common pattern of evangelical faith and practice.

In the Southern Region

The awakening movement had direct effects in the south. With the arrival of Baptists and Presbyterians in Virginia and the Carolinas, there was a strong challenge to Anglican hegemony. The Anglican churches' officials took steps at once to prevent the itinerant, revivalist ministers from evangelizing.

However, the awakening movement instilled in Baptists a new spirit of evangelical Calvinism. The new, alternative form that involved the popularization of new models of intimate Christian fellowship replaced the old, external religious observances in the southern regions.

It accelerated the splintering of American Protestantism by stimulating divisions in existing denominations; Congregationalists and Presbyterians were split into supporters and opponents of the new spirit.

It also stimulated the growth of new religious groups such as the Baptists, whose numbers had been insignificant before the Great Awakening.

The Awakening Movement Weakened Traditional Church Authority

The revivals encouraged converted laypeople to judge the spiritual qualifications of their ministers and induced parishioners to seek spiritual nourishment elsewhere if they wished to do so. Under certain circumstances, it appeared that ordinary people could express their opinions of their churches' religious superiors.

Under the new social mobility and equality, the awakening also gave huge energy to colonial society with the liberty and virtue applied to spiritual realities in the mid-eighteenth century.

Historical Conversions and Mobilization of the Laity

The awakening movement brought countless converts to the churches and had a monumental effect on the people, not just the churches, in colonial history. It quickened the spiritual interest of church people as well as the general public.

Waves of evangelicalism swept over the colonies from the late 1730s as some evangelical preachers insisted on the spiritual equality of all people and denied any kind of cultural differences based on origin, class, race, or gender.

They advocated that all colonial people—small farmers as well as craftsmen (masters and journeymen)—could participate in their pursuit of religious experience in the churches. The new breeze of spirit that spread across the colonies encouraged ordinary people and slaves to actively participate in evangelical religion; this provided rural Americans a common language thereby mitigating differences between ethnic groups.

The awakening also kindled interest in spreading the gospel among Native Americans. John Sargent and later Edwards ministered to Native Americans, and Eleazar Wheelock transformed his Indian Charity School into Dartmouth College.

The Awakening Shaped Colonial Culture

As the awakening moved across the colonies, the spiritual and cultural influences of the church community on the religious and social life of the country were very profound; missionary, educational, and humanitarian activities were greatly mobilized.

The spiritual movement had no doubt freed the colonies from their European religious roots; it created internal divisions among the Dutch Reformed, the Presbyterians, and the Congregationalists.

> But, paradoxically, it was at the same time a great force, transcending colonial and denominational barriers as nothing in America had done before. The explanation is that the revival ignored many of the old alignments based on theology and church government, and created new alignments by making personal conversion the supreme test question. Thus the way was prepared for the pragmatic ignoring of theoretical questions in favor of direct experience and practical results that was to become popular in America. But during the Great Awakening only a start was made in this direction.

Edwards declared that the Great Awakening was "a surprising work of God." Preachers such as Whitefield and Tennent preached to thousands by breaking the audiences' denominational boundaries and labels.

The Great Awakening is a historic religious revival movement that swept through the American colonies from 1735 to 1745. It was marked by sensational public repentances and conversions. It began from Massachusetts under the influence of the preaching of Edwards and Whitefield. Religious practices such as conversion became a matter of choice.

> Charismatic ministers, who lacked the scruples of Gilbert Tennent or Jonathan Edwards, ignored traditional boundaries in setting out to win souls-but in turn, if they were successful in setting up a new congregation which hearkened to their message, they found themselves prisoners or servants of their enthusiasts who were their means of support. Freelance preachers are not often much concerned with financial survival, which can be an unhealthy preoccupation. Priorities in worship changed in the Awakenings. Renewal was experienced as renewal of enthusiasm rather than performance of an unchanging liturgy; Protestant Churches which did not adapt, and which based themselves on traditional European models, suffered. The Anglicans, strongly linked to the Church of England, which was struggling at the same time with the Methodist and Evangelical Revivals were even more resistant than the Congregationalist Churches of New England to the style of the Awakenings.

Denominationalism Emerged

Denominationalism as it emerged from the Great Awakening eased sectarian antagonisms, but in the process, the cleavage between emotion and intellect widened.

The seventeenth-century brand of Protestantism brought

to the colonies from England appealed both to the head and the heart. But the awakeners, though generally educated men aware of theological subtleties willingly discarded the intellectual structure of Protestantism in their eagerness to gather in uncharted territory. Charles Chauncy, minister of the First Church in Boston, saw that the awakening's emotional appeal for converts opened the way for a fervent anti-intellectualism in the churches. Chauncy argued heatedly with Edwards in sermons and pamphlets against the awakening.

> In their notable debate, Chauncy has been pictured as the embodiment of the Enlightenment's ideals, which he was, and thus the Awakening in turn has been pictured as antithetical to the ideals of the Enlightenment, which it was-ultimately. Anti-intellectualism did in time come to dominate American Protestantism, but in the Eighteenth century, awakeners the enlightened for the most part consciously overlooked or failed to notice their divergent views toward life and worked together toward goals they shared in common.

The Wild Frontier Society Was Christianized

Early missionary drives also began to emerge. The awakening movement had achieved what the Anglicans had failed to in the ministry to slaves. The new spirit of evangelical demands for personal choice granted dignity to African immigrants who had never been offered a choice in their lives. It affected not only the institution of religion (the structure of existing churches) but also the social structure as well as thousands of converted, and it affected social conditions.

The Great Awakening also led to an increased interest in missionary work among the Native Americans as evidenced in

Whitefield's founding of the orphanage in Georgia.

Motivated by the Whitefield's ministry, many preachers followed in his footsteps. They started their own ministries across the colony with the result that many wild frontiers were reached for the first time. This was the indirect impact of Whitefield's ministry.

Relationship between the American Enlightenment and the Great Awakening

Colonial America was shaped by two forces that remained somewhat unreconciled to this day. The first was the influence of the Enlightenment, and the second was the force of the Great Awakening.

The main idea of the eighteenth-century Enlightenment originated in France. It proclaimed that all were born free and equal and all forms of religion should be tolerated and have freedom of expression. Enlightenment thinkers emphasized the primacy of reason and nature. They believed that all that could be known was already present in nature and that the way to knowledge was through the application of human reason to nature via the scientific method; this contrasted with the evangelical Protestant view.

Under the influence of the European Enlightenment, the people of colonial America believed that education played a vital role in their lives. The awakening movement was the first example in colony life of revivalism. It was a spiritual movement reacting against the rationalism and secularism of the Enlightenment. The Enlightenment provided the rational support against British rule over the colony, and the Great Awakening undermined traditional religious authority. At the dawn of the awakening movement, the church in the colonies had lost its vitality and ability to attract people to worship at church.

The Changing Wind of Religion and the Force of the Great Awakening

The Pilgrims and Puritans came to the colonies for religious freedom; they set strict moral standards of religious practice. They were convinced theirs was the true faith and did not tolerate others.

Their arrogance was first challenged by the outspoken Anne Hutchinson and later by Roger Williams. Other European religious denominations that migrated to the colonies before the awakening era added to the diversity of the new arrivals' populations, and religious tolerance became an unavoidable issue.

Contributions from the awakening movement under the democratizing of religion brought into the ministry less-educated clergymen. Four colleges—Brown (Baptist), Princeton (Presbyterian), Dartmouth (Congregational), and Rutgers (Dutch Reformed)—were founded to fill the educational void in the Great Awakening.

The revival gave tremendous power to people to challenge popular culture in the name of reason and religion but not in a way that advocated revolution as the Enlightenment did later. The Enlightenment movement mainly stressed reason and order; its influence on the elite New England colleges was passed on to church communities as well.

The confrontation between the Great Awakening and the Enlightenment was very complicated; within churches, however, the awakening was far more helpful than was the Enlightenment when it came to the nourishing of humanity's spiritual needs.

The relationship between revival and Enlightenment was therefore remarkably close. John Fletcher, Wesley's longtime lieutenant, argued "not only that feeling and rational Christianity are not incompatible, but also that such feeling, so far from deserving to be called madness and enthusiasm, are nothing short of the acting of spiritual life. Emotion, fervor, even irrationality, is inseparable from the human condition, but progressive opinion in the eighteenth century kept them bridled. So did evangelicals, investigating them in a dispassionate spirit of scientific enquiry. Such analysts were firmly bound up in the Enlightenment.

The Sovereignty of God and the Free Will of Humanity

God has full sovereignty over nature and history. Who dares to challenge His authority in the universe and on the earth He made? "The Lord has established His throne in heaven, and His kingdom rules over all" (Psalm 103:19).

Edwards was well known for his honoring the sovereignty of God: "The revealed will of God is the only perfect law of liberty, but how little is it believed and obeyed by Mankind."

Here is St. Augustine's statement regarding free will.

> God created man in His own image, man ought to know Him and it would only be natural for man to return to God." After the Fall of Man, the Lord made garments of skin for Adam and his wife and clothed them ... God allows nothing to remain unordered and ... knows all things before they come to pass. Nor are we dismayed by difficulty that what we chose to do freely is done of necessity, because He whose foreknowledge cannot be deceived foreknew that we would choose to do it ... We do not deny, of course, an order of causes in which the will of God is all-powerful. On the other hand, we do not give this order the name fate. However, our main point is that, from the fact that to God the order of all causes is certain, there is not [a] logical deduction that there

> is no power in the choice of you will. [The fact of the matter is that] our choices fall within the order of the causes which is known for certain to God and is contained in His foreknowledge-for human choices are the cause of human acts ... [Thus,] absolutely all bodies are subject to the will of God; as, indeed, are all wills, too, since they have "no power save what He gave them" and He knows exactly what they will do with it ... Our conclusion is that our wills have the power to do all that God wanted them to do and foreknew that they could do. Their power, such as it is a real power.

"And He is before all things, and by Him all things consist" (Colossians 1:17). Paul said, "All possible existences are included." Owing their existence to Christ, they are all subordinate to Him.

It is our duty to offer praise that glorifies God for "Honor and majesty are before Him; Strength and beauty are in His sanctuary" (Psalm 96:6).

What's the worldly philosophic view of free will? The traditional view of free will is, only those who have free will can be held morally responsible for what they do. Accordingly, if we are morally responsible, we have free will. This traditional view is held not only by those who think we do not have free will. Some holders of the traditional view assert both our moral responsibility and our free will. Others believe that because we do not have free will, we cannot be held morally responsible for our actions.

Unfortunately, the philosophers expressed only half the truth of free will; they pointed out also that it was important to keep the issue of moral responsibility separate from the issue of free will. Then they are getting rid of the responsibility to do whatever they want and follow their free will.

St. Augustine wrote in his *Confessions,*

The cause of evil is the free judgment of the will. But I also, as yet, although I said and was firmly persuaded, that Thou our Lord, the true God, who maddest not only our souls but our bodies, and not our souls and bodies alone, but all creatures and all things, were uncontainable and inconvertible, and in no part mutable, yet understood I not readily and clearly what was the cause of evil. And yet, whatever it was, I perceived that it must be so sought out as not to constrain me by it to believe that the immutable God was mutable, lest I myself should become the thing that I was seeking out. I sought, therefore, for it free from care, certain of the untruthfulness of what these asserted, whom I shunned with my whole heart; for I perceived that through seeking after the origin of evil, there were filled with malice, in that they liked better to think that Thy Substance did suffer evil than that their own did commit it. But again I said: "Who made me? Was it not my God, who is not only good, but goodness itself? Whence came I then to will to do evil, and to be unwilling to do good, that there might be cause for my just punishment? Who was it that put this in me, and implanted in me the root of bitterness, seeing I was altogether made by my most sweet God? If the devil were the author, whence is that devil? And if he also, by his own perverse will, of a good angel became a devil, whence also was the evil will in him whereby he became a devil, seeing that the angel was made altogether good by that most good Creator? By these reflections was I again cast down and stifled; yet not plunged into that hell of error (where no man confessed unto thee), to think that Thou dost suffer evil, rather than that man doth it. We shall praise the Lord for His holiness and grace by the divine authority created Adam after the image of God. It is not about me matter anymore; it is only matter for me to surrender my will to Him!

While the Great Awakening in the colonies was still in progress in 1741, it became divided over theological issues later referred to as the Calvinist–Arminian debate. Though the issues were age-old, the proponents of divine sovereignty were classed with the sixteenth-century Reformer of Geneva, John Calvin, and the advocates of human free will with the Dutch theologian of the early seventeenth century, Jacob Arminius. John Wesley's sermon against Calvinist predestination, "Free Grace" (1740), elicited a letter from George Whitefield, stating that he wrote with "unspeakable Sorrow of Heart" and was aware that some would be "offended" at his letter, others would rejoice, and still others would wish "this matter had never been brought under debated.

The issue of free will started when Adam fell; it constituted a breach of trust between God and humankind. The spiritual separation (the death of the human spirit after the likeness of God) resulted in the curse and eternal damnation.

Romans 5:15 reads, "But the free gift is not like the offense. For if by the one man's offense many died, much more the grace of God and the gift by the grace of the one Man, Jesus Christ, abounded to many."

The Testimony of Edwards and Whitefield Matters Today

Edwards's spiritual insight was his emphasis on the need for the American church to study: *"History* is His [God's] story; mine is treasures and you won't be disappointed." Edwards's penetrating insights were unmatchable; he wrote hundreds of papers defending and analyzing the awakening. He was called "the theologian of the hearts."

He was not only a pastor to his congregation members but also a counselor at his home gatherings at all times. His sermons never skipped the solemn question of heaven or hell. His writings encouraged readers to search for the truth of the beauty of God, enhanced the concepts of eternity, and transformed the purpose of church ministry that glorified God.

Edwards preached the sovereign, omnipotent, omniscient God who is gracious and good beyond human comprehension. His favorite adjective for God was *sweet*.

The mission of the church is proclaiming the gospel of the magnificent salvation of God. Scriptures made it clear in the Great Commission (Matthew 28:18–20). Following Jesus' resurrection, He instructed His disciples to go and make disciples of all nations and baptize them "in the name of the Father and of the Son and of the Holy Spirit." Much of the New Testament (Acts particularly) illustrates how God carried His plan through the power of the Holy Spirit mandating that the churches to fulfill this Great Commission.

Whitefield wrote in his journal, "We can preach the Gospel of Christ no further than we have experienced the power of it in our own hearts." Since God is the author and finisher of all His saints' faith, He is the master who mandates the ministers who were called and anointed them with the Holy Spirit. "For he whom God has sent speaks the words of God, for God does not gives the

Spirit by measure" (John 3:34).

Faithful preachers such as Edwards and Whitefield remind me of God's words in Isaiah 61:1: "The Spirit of the Lord is upon me, because the Lord has anointed me to preach good tidings to the poor. He has sent me to heal the brokenhearted, to proclaim liberty to the captives, and the opening of the prison to those who are bound."

True Religion and Conversion

> Edwards inherited his interest in practical religion from the Puritans, but the revivals raised the question of how to distinguish genuine religion from the false. He sought to answer this question by establishing clear signs for the former. In true religion, he said, the witness of the Spirit is manifest both in the exercises of grace within the heart and in outward practice. True conversion is evident from the presence of both faith and love within the person.

The conversion is the work of Spirit through the gospel of preachers who released the power from God on converts; they engaged in the marvelous process of turning sinners to God. The apostle Paul said it well: "I planted the seeds, and Apollo watering it, and the Holy Spirit made it grow!"

Edwards's Ministry Confirmed the Works of the Spirit of God

The history Edwards faced during the revivals at the Northampton Church (1734–35) gave him the observation of the fruits of revivals. He wrote in "Religious Affections" (1746), "More than 300 souls were saintly brought home to Christ."

> Yet, several occurrences marred the orderly work of the Spirit. In a state of spiritual despondence, Edwards's uncle committed suicide. Two people in nearby towns went mad with strange enthusiastic delusions. Others broke into laughter, tears at the same time issuing like a flood, and intermingling a loud weeping."

Parting from these incidents, Edwards in his *Faithful Narrative* and *Distinguishing Marks of a Work of the Spirit of God* (1741) defended the revivals as the genuine conversion and as the result by the God through the Holy Spirit.

The Spiritual Fruits of the Revivals

The proclamation of the true gospel converted many people in and outside church and made them members of God's big family. Before the awakening, the low tide of spiritual conditions in colonial churches had struck the hearts of many servants and brought out their desire for the Word of the Lord.

When the Holy Spirit manifested God's presence, many across the colonies witnessed the growth of the church. God prepared Edwards to be the theologian of revival; He sent Whitefield to preach the gospel to hundreds of thousands who did not have access to churches.

Our nation was in desperate need of a spiritual awakening before it was too late; the crisis of confusion of culture against God in our nation today reminds me of the curses of disobedience our nation will face. Deuteronomy 28:28 reads, "The Lord will strike you with madness and blindness and confusion of the heart."

Edwards was a firm believer in corporate prayer. He wanted Christians to become one body in Christ that would supplicate the almighty God collectively rather than individually. For the better part of time in colonial life, the Bible was far more accepted by the people. The spiritual revival movement could not happen anytime without the power of the Holy Spirit's intervention.

The unique element of the awakening movement was that God called strong preachers to proclaim the truth of the Scriptures, and they were faithful to God's commandments. As Edwards was the theologian of the time through his writing, he was a powerful influence then and later. Whitefield was a great and powerful orator who was able to move listeners deeply with his sermons. John Wesley was an administrative genius who established an extremely effective small group form of classic meetings that kept the fire of revival burning.

What our church needs today is the regeneration of a spiritual condition beginning with the feeding God's words.

The Passing of the Spiritual Revival's Baton

One of the main reasons the Great Awakening spread across the colonies was due to the passions it aroused in thousands; it created controversy among many churches regarding the question of the genuine nature of this awakening. Many churches' ministers opposed the revival; they were known as Old Lights, while those who supported it were known as New Lights.

As the awakening controversies mounted, many church members began to take sides. As a result of the arguments, many left their churches and founded independent churches. Baptists, Methodists, and many other denominations were created.

The Believers' Duty of Obedience to the Lord's Commands

The gospel is the grace God gave to humanity; it is the chance to gain forgiveness through Christ's crucifixion. The incarnation of the Son of God is the greatest gift He gave to the world.

"Though he was a Son, yet he learned obedience by the things which he suffered. And having been perfected, He became the author of eternal salvation to all who obey him" (Hebrews 5:8–9).

When Jesus was raised from the dead, the hearts of men were shaken and history was changed. The disciples moved from fear to joy and willingly accepted the divine mission to bring the gospel to the whole earth so all might become the Lord's people. The desire for the Lord drew followers to Jesus.

Religious testimony is every true believer's personal witness of the salvation power of God: "Come and hear, all you who fear God, and I will declare what He has done for my soul" (Psalm 66:16). The power of the Holy Spirit works to fulfill the vow that leads to public praise and witness of God's salvation. Such is the case of the Great Awakening in colonial America in the eighteenth century.

The Epoch-Making Era of the Great Awakening

Though the awakening produced no lasting effects on colonial religious life, it reached more people than did the Enlightenment. Laypeople continued to defer to their traditional ministers. The public turned out to welcome eloquent preachers such as Whitefield and Edwards with an enthusiastic spirit.

Edwards's and Whitefield's legacies demonstrated their faith; their walks in testimony of Christ confirmed many converts' life-changing experiences. They proclaimed the divinity of the gospel; God's Word empowered and touched countless souls during the Great Awakening. They were "enrich[ed] in everything by Him in all utterance and all knowledge" (1 Corinthians 1:5).

As the result of many evangelists led by Edwards and Whitefield, history was made in that awakening era. "Even as the testimony of Christ was confirmed in you" (1 Corinthians 1:6). Many lives were changed; believers testified to this years after the awakening.

> The leaders of the Awakening knew what they were after when they enlisted affective rhetoric to preach about intractable human depravity and supernal divine grace. They were trying to reawaken the church for the sake of the church itself in multiple ways. Their aim was to reassert the sovereignty of God's divine love in conversion, to exalt the substitutionary, penal work of Christ as God's way of reconciliation with sinners, to demonstrate the necessity of conversion as a prerequisite for truly virtuous living, and by these means to check the worldliness promoted by the era's new forms of commerce and entertainment. Yet the pursuit of such goals had ironic consequences. The awakeners preached a higher, more spiritual vision of the church, yet the result was a decline in the very notion of church and a transfer of religious commitment from the church to the nation.

The awakening movement obeyed our Lord's Great Commission by reaching out to the poor, to slaves who had been spurned by established sects, to all newly settled people, and to women, who were drawn to the new preaching available to them.

God cannot tolerate humanity's evil and iniquity. We cannot achieve heaven with sin on us. We require God's mercy for the forgiveness of our sins. With the atonement of the blood of the Lamb, we are born again.

Our Lord gave His disciples the promise of the Comforter, the Holy Spirit in John 16:13: "However, when He, the Spirit of truth, has comes, He will *guide* you into all truth; for He will not speak on his own authority, but whatever He hears He will *speak*; and He will *tell* you things to *come*." Edwards and Whitefield guided listeners to all truth, including the warnings from the Lord to repent and be baptized in the name of the Lord before the judgment comes.

At the peak of the awakening era, newspapers devoted front pages to revival stories and turned the revival preachers' travels into daily headline events. Benjamin Franklin was fascinated by the charisma of Whitefield and followed his exploits in his newspapers. Once, when a crowd filled the Market Square of downtown Philadelphia to listen to Whitefield's testimony, Franklin estimated there were around 30,000 people in attendance.

Edwards's and Whitefield's warning voices were echoed throughout the churches of the New England region and across the colony for the repentance and obedient of the commandments of God's command. Edwards and Whitefield testimonies had to have been the irrepressible works of the Holy Spirit.

Our nation today is facing a serious crisis; it is drifting from the founding fathers' vision to be a nation that honors God and praises Him for all His blessings. Praise the Lord for the evangelists in the Great Awakening who planted the seeds of the desired Word of God; they turned their hearers back to the Bible.

Many colonial Christians in and since the Great Awakening have decorated their family rooms with biblical verses and read from family Bibles.

Under the leadership of Edwards and Whitefield, many other preachers achieved unprecedented milestones in Christian history. That their efforts met with considerable success is revealed in data on the church's founding.

> In the period 1710–40, the member of churches in Massachusetts increased from 87 to 207, and the number of churches in Connecticut from 46 to 120.

> In the span of one generation, 194 churches were founded in the two colonies; more than a quadruple of each of three generations had average. So phenomenal was the growth rate of the church that it exceeded the growth rate of population, which itself was phenomenal.

The Great Awakening is credited for bridging the yawning cultural gap between African Americans and European Americans, edifying local revivalists, and evangelizing colonial churches. The spiritual revival movement touched the hearts of thousands of people as did the Great Awakening on the continent. It was beyond the human finite brains' to imagine. It had not happened before the Great Awakening; that is what made the movement so great!

> Puritan professionalism also involved ministers in a transatlantic evangelic network, one with deep roots in the seventeenth-century Dissenting network thrown up by the Puritan "community of saints," through this network evangelical ministers shared ideas and news about revival that, in the 1740s, crystallized into the modern notion of the great and general revival.

Such is the example of the Great Awakening movement. Edwards and Benjamin Colman of New England entered a letter-writing network with James Robe, William McCulloch, and John McCulloch of Scotland and Isaac Watts and Whitefield of England. By the communications among the preachers, this new, international epistolary circuit promoted the process of convergence in the circles of evangelicalism.

Amazing Hand of the Lord

Whitefield was rejected by the Church of England for his outdoor ministry. It was a miracle even beyond Whitefield's thought that God used Whitefield's ministry to enlarge the kingdom of God in colonial America. Susan O'Brien wrote,

> The major contrast that historians have drawn between the spontaneity of the mid-eighteenth-century revivals and the professionalism of those in the nineteenth century is misleading ... Instead, the eighteenth-century revivals should take their place on a continuum of Protestant evangelical development. The real significance of the mid-eighteenth-century revivals was not their wondrous spontaneity or their primary role in the formation of a national consciousness, but rather their combining of traditional Puritan practices with fresh evangelical techniques and attitude.

Charles G. Finney reported,

> It swept over the land with such power that an estimated 50,000 or more conversions were hard to make since the number of meeting's increased so rapidly and since "all classes of people were inquiring everywhere, slavery seemed to shut it out from the South. The people there were in such a state of irritations, of vexation, and of committed to their peculiar institution, that the Spirit of God seemed to be grieved away from them."

Walter A. McDougall commented in his Book of *Freedom Just around the Corner,*

> Should the term "Great Awakening" be purged in favor of some complex sentence to the effect that the 1730s witnessed new forms of mass

evangelization that may or may not have quickened the spirituality of one generation of American colonists? Not quite-and not only because of the revival's effects, construction suggests something profound about the gestation of American culture. By praying for the land to be scorched by the Spirit, but at the same time acting as if *God needed their help* to do His surprising works; by calling the country to emotional, transcendental rebirth, while at the same time blessing its rational, material order, preachers and converts alike were living the millenarian hopes entertained by Mather and Edwards. They were, if only subconsciously, thrusting their clutches skyward to pull down heaven itself-down to America. You can't help but do well and feel good about it, in heaven.

The study of the Great Awakening has to deal with two sides of a coin: the opposition and dissension it produced, and the overall churches' condition before and after the awakening. The awakening gave new life to the churches; it led to the rapid growth of Presbyterians and Baptists and led to the formation of the Methodists.

The Religious Revival Was the Important Factor behind Social Progress

The awakening elevated ordinary people socially.

By giving the common people a self-authenticating religious experience it made him independent of professional ministers and church synods. Lay activity and lay authority in the church increased. It was only a step to apply This new significance of the individual and his new experience in leadership to the political sphere where it further stimulated the burgeoning democracy.

John Wesley wrote that God's law was a witness between God and humanity. He gave a clearer comment about these two verses from Psalm 19.

> The law-The doctrine delivered to his church, whether by Moses, or by other prophets, having discoursed hither of the glory of God shining forth in, the visible heavens. God's law is a witness between God and man; faithful or true, which is most necessary in a witness.

The Blessed of God's Nation

"Blessed is the nation whose God is the Lord, the people whom he has chosen as his heritage!" (Psalm 33:12). "God is the One who initiated the relationship with Israel, the nation he chose" (Deuteronomy 7:7–11).

The Puritans sailed from England to seek the freedom in religion to worship the Lord. We are the chosen nation because the Lord loves the descendants of our founding fathers, who honored God and followed the teachings of the Bible.

The "Vow and Contract" part of the Declaration of Independence included words from Deuteronomy (15:17–21) and Leviticus 25:35–36). For our nation to turn back to God, we have to heed the words of Isaiah 1:16: "Wash yourselves, make yourselves clean, put away the evil of your doings from before my eyes; Cease to do evil."

Repentance

True repentance is the fruit of the Holy Spirit; it begins with the

Word of God. It is a change of choice, intention, and purpose in conformity with the dictation of a person's intelligence. It works to turn a sinner's heart from sin to holiness, and it brings a change of mind, the repentance that is required of all sinners.

Our nation is rebelling against God. "An evil man seeks only rebellion, therefore a cruel messenger will be sent against him" (Proverbs 17:11). God warned us in Proverbs 27:4, "Wrath is cruel, and anger a torrent, but who is able to stand before jealousy?"

Testimonies Must Confirm the Work of the Spirit

Our conscience is enlightened by the Spirit of God through the sanctification of the Word of God. This is illustrated in 2 Corinthians 1:12: "For our boasting is this, the testimony of our conscience that we conducted ourselves in the world in simplicity and godly sincerity, not with fleshly wisdom but by the grace of God, and more abundantly toward you."

By the early 1740s, Edwards was having his greatest success as an awakener outside of his own congregation. Conversely, the greatest success in Northampton occurred under sermons by a guest preacher. In early 1742, the young minister Samuel Buell filled Edwards's pulpit while Edwards was away on a preaching tour and raised the revival spirit to dizzying heights. Edwards's wife, Sarah, experienced her most dramatic religious rapture under Buell's preaching. She described her experience as follows:

> That night [January 28, 1742] ... was the sweetest night I ever had ... The great part of the night I lay awake; sometimes asleep, and sometimes between sleeping and walking. I seemed to myself to perceive a glow of divine love come down from the heart of Christ in heaven, into my heart, in a constant stream, like a stream or pencil of sweet light." On

the next day, Sarah Edwards wrote, "I felt a love to all mankind, wholly peculiar in its strength, and sweetness, far beyond all that I had ever felt before." Jonathan Edwards endorsed Sarah Edwards's revival experience by including an altered version of her spiritual narrative in Some Thoughts Concerning the Revival (with Sarah's gender and identity concealed), and then capping off his presentation on her experience with the word: "Now if such things are enthusiasm, and the fruits of a distempered brain, let my brain be evermore possessed of that happy distemper!"

Is It Too Late to Pray for Our Nation's Revival?

No. It is not a question of who is right or wrong; it is a matter of starting to get right with God. One by one, starting with every believer in his or her home church, for the kingdom of God, we need to come together for corporate prayer and plead for forgiveness of our sins and those of the nation. The United States, my beloved country, needs a new birth.

> The new birth is, then, a sovereign act of God by his Spirit in which the believer is cleansed from sin and given spiritual birth into God's household. It renews the believer's intellect, sensibility, and will to enable that person to enter the kingdom of God and to do good works. The Old Testament saints were born again when they responded in faith to God's revealed message; New Testament saints when they respond in faith to Jesus Christ.

It will be a glorious time when people shall be converted to God; God will certainly make it yield them an abundance of spiritual fruit. God made it known to His chosen people that they were the chosen race; God's covenant was given to the seed of Abraham; that pointed to Christ. God is pleased with his peculiar people (1 Peter 2:9 and all the born-again Christians who witness to other people are welcome into the house of the Lord, the church, and can share the new covenant of God's great love!

Watchman duty is God's sacred calling to all evangelists and children to watch, pray, be steadfast during trials and tribulations, and wait for the second coming of our Lord.

Renewed Purity in Fighting Spiritual Battles

Resist Satan and have your mind set against him. "But put on the Lord Jesus Christ, and make no provision for the flesh, to fulfill its lust" (Romans 13:14). Jesus used the Word of God to thwart Satan's attempts against Him (Matthew 4:1–11). Meditate daily on God's Word in your devotional time. "Your word I have hidden in my heart, that I might not sin against You" (Psalm 119:11).

We should submit ourselves to God as James 4:8 said: "Draw near to God and He will draw near to you. Cleanse your hands, you sinners; and purify your hearts, you double-mined." The key to overcoming evil is to submit ourselves to God. When we come close to God, He will draw near to us. This begins with confessing our sins and submitting to God wholeheartedly. Watch, pray, and wait for our Lord patiently till His second coming. May You come quickly, O my Lord and Savior!

Romans 1:16 tells us, "For I am not ashamed of the gospel of Christ, for it is the power of God to salvation for everyone who believes, for the Jew first and also for the Greek." I am certain it is not too late for us to pray together for our nation's revival and willingly and faithfully honor God and obey His Commandments.

FINAL THOUGHTS

The influences on the lives of Edwards and Whitefield have their roots in the depth of their compassion for humanity. Every believer's life is a living testimony to God's provision in Philippians 4:19: "And my God shall supply all your need according to His riches in glory by Jesus Christ."

We know our awesome God through His love: "Beloved, let us love one another, for love is of God; and everyone who loves is born of God and knows God" (1 John 4:8). "Of His own will He bring us forth by the word of truth, that we might be a kind of first-fruits of His creatures" (James 1:18).

"Praise the Lord," George Whitefield said. "Christ was God and man in one person, that God and man might be happy together again." Edwards and Whitefield followed the footsteps of Jesus to faithfully fulfill the Great Commission. As faithful servants of God, they were not afraid to condemn those who taught falsehoods. They stayed on the true path of Jesus till the end. Their testimonies and legacies will always be remembered.

In the late eighteenth century, George Washington said, "Religion and morality were indispensable supports to our political prosperity." John Adams said, "Our Constitution was made only for moral and religious people. It is wholly inadequate to the government of any other."

Jesus said, "As long as it is day, we must do the works of him who sent me. Night is coming, when one can work" (John 9:4).

Arise, shine, for your light has come, and the glory of the Lord rises upon you. See, darkness covers the earth and thick darkness is over the peoples, but the Lord rises upon you and his glory appears over you. (Isaiah 60:1–2)

May God have mercy upon our nation and all His children, amen!

BIBLIOGRAPHY

Armstrong, Chris. *Trouble with George* (January 2010), http://Christianhistory.net.

Armstrong, Karen. *A History of God*. New York: Roman Catholic Church of Maryland House. August 9, 1994.

Bailey, Richard. *"Devoted Disciplinarian,"* in *Christian History Magazine* (January 1, 2003), http://www.christianHistory.net.

Balmer, Randall and Lauren E. Winner. *Protestantism*. New York: Columbia University Press, November 2005.

Beeke, Joel R. *Forerunner of the Great Awakening: Sermons by Rev. Theodorus J. Frelinghuysen: 1691–1747*. Eerdmans, 2000.

Blake, William D. *Almanac of the Christian Church*. Bethany House, 1987.

Blumhofer, Edith L. and Randall Ballmer. *Modern Christian Revivals*. University of Illinois Press, 1993.

Brauer, Jerald C. *Protestantism in America*. Westminster Press, 1965.

Broderick, Robert C. *Catholic Encyclopedia*. Vatican. Rome. 1976.

Butler, Jon. *Religion in American Life*. Oxford University Press, 2007.

Buttrick, David. *Homiletic*. Fortress Press, 1987.

Cairns, Earle. *Christianity through the Centuries*. Zondervan, 1954.

Carman, Harry J. and Harold C. Syrett. *A History of the American*

People. New York: McClelland & Stewart, 1952.

Catholic University of America. *New Catholic Encyclopedia*. Washington, D.C.: Catholic University of America, 2003.

Cherry, Conrad. *The Theology of Jonathan Edwards*. Indiana University Press, 1990.

Christian History Institute. *Christian History Magazine 38* (April 1, 1993), http://christianhistoryinstitude.org.

Cosgrove, Mark P. *Foundation of Christian Thought*. Kregel Academic & Professional, 2006.

Curnock, Nehemiah, editor. *The Journal of the Rev. John Wesley*, A.M. London: Epworth Press, 1938.

Dallimore, Arnold A. George Whitefield. *Crossway Books*, 1990.

Dallimore, Arnold A. Whitefield: *Life and Times of the Great Evangelist of the 18th Century Revival*. Banner of Truth, 1980.

Davis, Emmalon. *Works of Jonathan Edwards,* volume 2 (Christian Classic Ethereal Library, 2010), http://www.ccel.org.

Davison, Elizabeth. *The Establishment of English Church in Continental American Colonies*. Duke University Press, 1936.

Doren, Carl Van. *Benjamin Franklin*. Viking Press, 1938.

Dowley, Tim. *Eerdmans's Handbook to the History of Christianity*. Eerdmans publishing Company, 1977.

Driscoll, Mark and Gering Breshears. *Doctrine: What Christians Should Believe*. Crossway Books, 2010.

Dwight, Sereno E. *Memoir of Jonathan Edwards*, A.M. Edward Hickman, 1834.

Edwards, Jonathan. *Works of Jonathan Edwards*, volume 1. Christian Classic Ethereal Library, 1998. http://www.ccel.org.

Edwards, Jonathan. *The Works of Jonathan Edwards*, volume 16. Letters and Personal Writings. Yale University Press, 1998.

Edwards, Jonathan. *History of Redemption*. Oxford University Press, 1776.

Edwards, Jonathan. *Sinners in the Hands of an Angry God*. Ligonier Ministries, http://www.ligonier.org.

Edwards, Jonathan. *Personal Narrative*. 2011. http://www.christianbook.com.

Edwards, Jonathan. *Surprising Work of God*. Jupiter Images, 2013.

Eerdmans, William. *Eerdmans's Handbook to the History of Christianity*. Eerdmans Pub Co, 1977.

Eidemuller, Michael E. *Speech Communication Texts*. Tyler: University of Texas. http://www.uttyler.edu.

Encyclopedia of Religion. *Macmillan Encyclopedia*, 2nd edition. 1986.

Farabaugh, Daniel. *United States History*. McGraw-Hill, 2012.

Finer, Eric. *Reader's Companion to American History*. Houghton Mifflin, 1991.

Finley, Samuel. *Christ Triumphing and Satan Raging in Great Awakening*, 1741.

Fullerton, W. Y. Church. *Biography of Charles H. Spurgeon Sermon from Pulpit Archive*. http:// http://www.cityvision.edu/wiki/charles-spurgeon.

Gaustad, Edwin Scott and Leigh E. Schmidt. *A Religious History of America*. Harper & Row, 2004.

Geisler, Norman. *Systematic Theology*, volume 1. Bethany House, 2003.

Goodwin, Gerald J. *A History of the United States*. Alfred A. Knopf, 1985.

Gura, Philip F. Jonathan Edwards. *Hill and Wang*. 2005.

Hammond, Peter. *Reformation Journal*. 1960. http://www.reformation.S.A.org.

Handy, Robert T. *A History of Church in the United Stated and Canada*. Cambridge University Press, 1979.

Hawke, David. *The Colonial Experience*. Bobbs-Merrill, 1966.

Haviland, William A. *Cultural Anthropology*. Wadsworth, 2013.

Haykin, Michael A. G. *The Life and Legacy of Jonathan Edwards*.

Toronto: Baptist Seminary, 2014.

Heimert, Alan and Perry Miller. *Great Awakening*. Bobbs-Merrill, 1967.

Helms, Paul. *Table Talk and Magazine*. Orlando, FL: Ligonier Ministries.

Hoch, Carl B. The New Birth. *Article written on Dictionary of Biblical Theology*. Walter A. Elwell, editor Baker Books.

Hopkins, Samuel. *Memoirs of Jonathan Edwards*. London: James Black, 1815.

Hudson, Winthrop S. *Religion in America*. Charles Scribner's Sons, 1965.

Jackson, Thomas, editor. *John Wesley's Sermon Text*. 1872. http://www.ccel.org.

Johnson, Paul. *History of Christianity*. Touchstone, 1976.

Johnson, Philip R. *The Hall of Church History. Theology from a Bunch of Dead Guys*. 2001, http://www.spurgeon-phil/wesley.htm.

Kraft, Charles H. *Anthropology for Christian Witness*. Maryknoll, NY: Orbis, 1996.

Landsman, Ned C. *From Colonial to Provincials*. Tyndale, 1997.

Lamsa, George M. *More Light on the Gospel*. Garden City, N.Y: Doubleday, 1968.

Lawson, Steven J. *Unwavering Resolute of Jonathan Edwards*. Orlando, FL: Ligonier Ministries, 2008.

Lovelace, Richard. *Edwards's Theology*. Christian History Institute quarterly 8 (1983).

MacCulloch, Diarmaid. *Christianity*. Viking, 2010.

McClymond, Michael J. and Gerald R. McDermott. *Theology of Jonathan Edwards*. Oxford University Press, 2012.

McDermott, Gerald R. *Great Theologians*. Intervarsity Press, 2010.

McDougall, Walton A. *Freedom Just around the Corner*. HarperCollins, 2004.

Elwell, Walter A. (editor). *Dictionary of Biblical Theology*. Baker

Books, 1996.

McGrath, Alister E. *Christian Theology*. Wiley-Blackwell, 2011.

McGrath, Alister E. *Christianity's Dangerous Idea*. HarperCollins, 2007.

McGrath, Alister E. *Historical Theology*. Oxford University Press, 1991.

Martineau, James. *Study of Religion*. Oxford: Clarendon Press, 1889.

Morrison, Samuel Eliot. *Oxford History of the American People*. Oxford: Oxford University Press, 1965.

Morrison, Samuel Eliot. *The Growth of the American Republic*. Oxford: Oxford University Press, 1980.

Niebuhr, Richard R. *Experiential Religion Book*. Harper & Row, 1972.

Nichols, James H. *History of Christianity: 1650–1950*.

Ronald Press, 1956. Noll, Mark A. *History of Christianity in the United States and Canada*. William B. Eerdmans, 1992.

Olson, Roger E. *Arminian Theology, Myths and Reality*. Intervarsity Press, 2006.

Olson, Roger E. *The History of Christian Theology*. Intervarsity Press, 1999.

Parley, William P. *Jonathan Edwards and the Great Awakening*. The General Council of the Assemblies of God, 2002.

Pikington, J. G. *The Confession of St. Augustine*. Jazzybee Verlag, 2016.

Pollock, John. *George Whitefield & Great Awakening*. Reformation Society Journals, http://www.reformationsa.org/index.php/history/78-gwhitefield.

Purvis, Thomas L. *Colonial America to 1763*. Facts on Files.

Reiley, Woodrige. *American Thought*. Henry Holt.

Riverside *Dictionary of Biography*. (George Whitefield) Houghton Mifflin.

Rusten, E. Michael and Sharon O. Rusten. *The One Year Christian*

History. Carol Stream: Tyndale, 2003.

Schaff, Philip. Person of Christ: *The Miracle of History*. Charles Scribner's.

Schmidt, Roger. *Patterns of Religion*. Cengage Learning, 2003.

Smith, John E. *A Jonathan Edwards's Reading*. New Haven: Yale University Press, 2003.

Smith, Shelton. *American Christianity*. New York Scribner's c, 1963.

Thomas, John L. *Religion and American People*. Westminster, MD: Newman Press, 1963.

Thornton, Mark. *Do We Have Free Will?* Bristol Classic, 1990.

Towns, Elmer L. *The Ten Great Revivals Ever. From Pentecost to the Present*. Liberty University. http:// http://digitalcommons.liberty.edu/towns_books/3. Wach, Joachim. Sociology of Religion. University of Chicago Press, 1944.

Wagner, C. Peter and Donald A. McGavran. Understanding Church Growth. Eerdmans, 1990.

Walton, Robert C. Church History. Grand Rapids: Zondervan, 2005.

Wheatley, Phillis. *An Elegiac Poem*. Boston: Russell and Boyles, 1770. Whitefield, George. *George Whitefield's Journals*. Quinta Press, 2000. http://www.quintapress.com.

Willimon, William H. and Richard Lischer, editors. *Concise Encyclopedia of Preaching*. Kentucky: Westminster John Knox Press, 1995.

Wills, Garry. *Head and Heart*. Penguin, 2007. WikiBooks. American Literature/Colonial Period: 1629–1776. 1959. http://www.wikibooks.org/wiki.

Zuckerman, Michael. *Peaceable Kingdoms*. Alfred A. Knopf, 1970.

VITA

I, Mark C. Lee, was born in Chengdu, China, in 1942. I grew up in Taiwan and came to United States in 1973. I studied at Long Island University, New York and was awarded a master's in sociology in 1974. I attained a master of ministry degree from the Vision University, a seminary, in 2009. God called me to the ministry of youth counseling first at the Harvest Church of Jersey City, NJ, from November 1998 to May 2011. He then called me to the Truth Church, a new missionary Lutheran Church from Taiwan, in Bayside, NY, as a part-time teacher from July 2012 to March 2013. I was appointed as the counsel for the youth ministry full-time from April 2013. I feel privileged to serve the Lord as a bilingual counselor for youth, and to bridge and strengthen the communication between children and parents. I am married and have three children and two grandchildren. I seek to inspire the people I meet in my evangelical work.

CONCISE CHRONOLOGY

1721 The conversion of Jonathan Edwards, the leading Calvinist theologians in colonial America.

1726 The beginning of the Great Awakening in colonial America.

1732 The thirteen colonies' first Roman Catholic Church of Maryland celebrated its premier in Philadelphia.

1735 George wrote to John Wesley of his conversion on May 7th.

1735 John Wesley, early Methodism's most influential leader, landed at Savannah, Georgia, as minister to an Anglican parish. He departed on December 7, 1737, after a grand jury charged him with defaming a parishioner's reputation by denying her communion.

1738 The conversion of John Wesley on May 24 as he and Charles prayed all night for salvation and his heart strangely warmed.

1739 Rev. George Whitefield, the man who's preaching sparked American's First widespread revival, the Great awakening, arrived in Philadelphia from England, and started preaching in Philadelphia (also in 1754, 1764, and 1770).

1741 Jonathan Edwards preaches on "Sinners in the Hands of an Angry God" on July 8th.

1742 The first school for girls, the Moravian Seminary for Women, was found at Bethlehem, Pennsylvania.

1743 John Wesley almost killed by a mob on October 20th.

1748 Conversion of John Newton working on a slave ship.

1758 Jonathan Edwards inoculated unsuccessfully against smallpox.

1770 George Whitefield's last sermon on September 29th.